Hamilton Aïdé

A Voyage of Discovery

Vol. II

Hamilton Aïdé

A Voyage of Discovery
Vol. II

ISBN/EAN: 9783337040321

Printed in Europe, USA, Canada, Australia, Japan

Cover: Foto ©ninafisch / pixelio.de

More available books at **www.hansebooks.com**

A VOYAGE OF DISCOVERY

A Novel of American Society

BY

HAMILTON AÏDÉ

IN TWO VOLUMES

VOL. II.

LONDON
JAMES R. OSGOOD, McILVAINE & CO.
45, ALBEMARLE STREET, W.
1892

[*All rights reserved*]

A VOYAGE OF DISCOVERY.

CHAPTER I.

A MAN who, in middle age, falls passionately in love, after many bitter disappointments, is as liable to do foolish things, in this same matter, as a raw youth of twenty. He is blind once more. Experience has taught him nothing; his hard cruel insight into the folly and weakness of others is now of no avail. It may be that he is deceived in the woman; or, as in this case, that his worldly wisdom unaccountably fails him just when it should be of most service to protect him from committing an irretrievable error.

It was strange that Ferrars should mistake the difference Miss Ballinger showed in her manner when talking to him and to other men, the keen alacrity with which she listened to, and the fearless manner in which she attacked, many of his views, for growing interest of a deeper kind. He misunderstood her character, if not completely, at all events, in part. No woman, he believed, could care so much to convert a man to her way of thinking, who was indifferent as to that man's future. She was not indifferent; this young woman felt an unusual, almost a passionate concern about the lives of those in whom she was interested; and she was sincerely interested in Quintin Ferrars. But it was not the sort of interest he imagined: therein was the initial error of his conduct towards her.

On his way from church that evening, he sounded Mrs. Courtly.

"Have you had much conversation with Miss Ballinger since she arrived?"

"No private conversation. Why?"

"I saw a great deal of her in New York. We met every day. Sometimes I was for hours virtually alone with her. You can guess the result as regards myself. I thought I could never care for a woman again. But I care about this English girl as I never cared before. Has she ever spoken to you about me?"

"Not since we were on board the *Teutonic*. She asked me then about you, but I told her nothing. I knew you disliked your secret being talked of, and, as it has been so well kept, I resolved to say nothing, unless absolutely forced to do so." Then, after a pause, "She is not a woman to be lightly won, Quintin."

"No; but—unless I am an ass—she takes that sort of interest in me which may deepen into—something stronger. What I want, on all accounts, is time. And that is just the difficulty. They will only be here a few days."

"Yes, they are going west, after passing a day or two in Boston, when their aunt arrives."

"And they will leave America in the spring. And if I follow them west, they will be staying with people I don't know. It is time you see, I want—time!"

"Do nothing precipitate, at all events. When will you be free?"

"Not for five months yet. Oh! my dear friend! It seems such an age now, before I can throw off those cursed bonds; and I had grown so indifferent to them! My life was blasted, and as long as I loved no other woman, it was all one to me. But now—"

He broke off with so deep a sigh that Mrs. Courtly was startled. All the way home he talked of this English girl, and of nothing else. His friend recognized no longer the man who for years had found so little in life to prize, to admire, or to love.

On their return home, they found Saul Barham. Mrs. Courtly had said nothing of his coming for the night; she had kept it as a little surprise for Grace, who would be pleased, she knew, to see him. And she was right. Miss Ballinger greeted the young professor with a warmth which made Quintin Ferrars jealous. He had never liked Barham. More than once on board the *Teutonic* their opinions, or something that lay deeper than opinions, had clashed. Ferrars, so trenchant in his judgments, found a man, fifteen years his junior, who treated him more than cavalierly; for hesitation and diffidence were not among Saul's weaknesses. The young Harvard Professor felt a certain contempt for this idle, wandering fellow-countryman of his, with his superior *nil admirari* tone about their common land; and he showed it. The greeting between the two, therefore, was cold, almost to freezing point, on this occasion; and Ferrars was sore at heart when he saw Grace's fair face beaming with smiles.

"How is your mother, to begin with?" she asked; and when reassured on that point, "Have you felt strong, yourself, since you returned to work? You look a little pale; not quite as well as you did after our six days' voyage."

"Of course not," he replied, smiling. "The Creation took six days. I was re-created during that voyage. I was another man. For the last two months I have been a worm again, grubbing in the earth, but, barring a real little cough, I am pretty well."

She thought him looking thin and worn, but said no more on the subject. She told him she meant to write to Mrs. Barham, and propose herself for an afternoon visit, as soon as she and her brother arrived in Boston.

"She will love to receive you, Miss Ballinger. She so often speaks of you to me. She would not venture to ask you to stay, but if any circumstance should render it possible for you to pass a few days under our roof, it would be a real joy to—us all."

"It would be nice, if I could manage it. Perhaps, if my brother goes to meet my aunt in New York, I may be able, for a couple of days—but I am afraid you won't be at home?"

"I can run down in the evenings to dine and sleep, and back to my work in Cambridge in the morning. I very often do it. It is no distance by rail. And I generally pass my Sunday at home. You will let me take you over Harvard College, I hope?"

"Certainly. I am looking forward to seeing Cambridge, which is associated in my mind with so many eminent men. You like your life there? You are happy?"

"I like my work; I know it is the best thing my hand can find to do, and I am told I do it successfully. Then I am in touch with men of congenial minds. But happy?" He paused, and looked out on the twilight deepening into night, with the fixed gaze in those large grey eyes which was so characteristic of him. "Happiness, I believe, depends greatly on physical conditions. I am not quite as strong as I should like to be. We have a splendid gymnasium. If I could take more athletic exercise than I do, I daresay I should have more even spirits."

Mrs. Courtly here joined them, and the little *tête-à-tête* was broken up. The lamps were brought in, the shutters closed. In the meantime Mrs. Planter, at the further end of the room, was questioning Sir Mordaunt as to the new guest whom Miss Ballinger appeared to know so well.

"Barham? I never heard of the name. It does not belong to any of our first families, anyhow."

"Well known in England," said Mordaunt, carelessly. "Ingoldsby Legends, you know."

"Do you mean there is any legendary lore connected with the Barhams? Well, they *may* have come over in the *Mayflower*, but I never heard them mentioned."

"No. I mean the author of 'The Jackdaw of Rheims,' and lots of other things, awfully good fun, you know, was a parson, named Barham."

"Oh! a minister—oh! And what is this young man?"

"A professor, I believe."

"He does not look like a well man. So *very*—"

"Yes, very," echoed Ballinger, impatiently. "But he makes up in brains, I am told, what he wants is flesh and muscle. My sister thinks a great deal of him. He is not my sort of man; rather a prig, I think; but people have different tastes. Now *she* couldn't bear Gunning, whom *I* thought not half a bad fellow."

"Jem Gunning is not very cultivated, I admit," said Mrs. Planter, authoritatively, as though cultivation and she were inseparable; "but he is *very* amiable."

"I don't think Grace cares for amiability alone," laughed her brother.

"Well, but—he *has* something else—one of our greatest *partis !*"

"That wouldn't affect her a bit. She is a queer girl."

"Looks to an alliance with your aristocracy, I conclude?"

He laughed again. "That is the last thing she would think of. I believe, Mrs. Planter, you think a great deal more of that, in America, than we do in England."

"Is that so? Well, I always say to Mr.

Planter, there's nothing like your aristocracy, Sir Mordaunt. I don't hold much to foreign nobility, but English, when one has once seen them in their home; ah! They are so *very*—"

"Right are you, Mrs. Planter. But hasn't foreign nobility a considerable value among you, too? Look at the fuss they made in New York with that young Marquis de Tréfeuille."

"Well, I always told my daughter that he did not amount to much, though his patent of nobility dates from Louis XV. Clare does not care for foreigners, anyway."

"I'm glad you don't count us as foreigners. After all, we have the same blood, haven't we? If we were Scotch, we *might* be relations. It is such rot, that jealousy between the two countries."

Had he been the most astute diplomatist, he could not have made a speech better calculated to please Mrs. Planter. She said to her daughter, as they dressed for dinner, that she had always liked Sir Mordaunt Ballinger, but she found him now really too nice for anything.

The beautiful Clare murmured something which was not very intelligible to her mother.

Indeed, her daughter's sentiments on this subject were not clear to her fond parent. The girl had been having "a good time" to-day, in almost uninterrupted flirtation with the English baronet. But Mrs. Planter attached no undue importance to this. She knew her daughter too well. Clare had all the wisdom of her countrywomen in the conduct of such affairs; she would never lose her head; she would never be led by vanity, or tenderness, or passion, to commit herself, until she was satisfied that this was the man, and none other, she ought and desired to marry. Herein she showed her superiority to the English girl, who becomes quickly intoxicated, loses all balance of judgment, and plights her troth in a flood of foolish words, which she often bitterly regrets. We are apt to call the American cold and heartless. She is not necessarily so, because she seems to be playing with a man, much as a cat does with a mouse. It may be that she is worldly and calculating; it may be that she is diverting herself at her adorer's expense. But there is the other possibility: she may be gauging, in the only way a woman can gauge, the man's character, and the measure of her liking for him. She does not succumb to his personal charm, to his fervent admiration, at once; she wants to know more of him, and, having very keen preceptions, builds up her knowledge from all the chance words he lets fall. It is true that she responds to his advances, that she "encourages" him, as we call it, more than custom approves in England; but she looks upon the game as a fair one, entailing, as she conceives, but small damage to either party. Ever since she was a little girl, she has known that man was a predatory animal, seeking whom he may devour. She has no idea of being devoured; least of all when she is a great heiress, fully conscious how many hunters are on her track. No! she will fight them with their own weapons, and when she yields, it will not be from ignorance of their vulnerable points.

In this case, Grace, who watched her brother's movements with keen interest, could not make up her mind how far either or both players were in earnest. Mordaunt had an unlimited capacity for flirtation; but under that thin surface of chaff and protestation with which he met the attack of every pretty woman, there were layers of susceptibility, which had more than once been pierced. This careless, impudent young Englishman, with all his faults, had a heart. It had been touched, though happily not very seriously, before now. But if this state of things went on for several days, and that the girl had a stronger head than her brother (which Grace never doubted), and was only amusing herself, how would it be with Mordaunt then? She had not seen enough of Clare Planter to determine whether she wished her for a sister-in-law; but she was quite sure she had no prejudice against her on the score of nationality. If the girl should care for him, and that her character was one likely to make him happy, Grace would further her brother's wishes by every means in her power.

Her reflections did not take this substantive form till Tuesday morning. The Sunday evening had been very pleasant to everyone but Ferrars. Burton had played, and Saul Barham had sat beside Grace, and a few words had passed now and again, during the intervals of the music. There was a bond of sympathy between them which, for the time being, required no other language. Mordaunt and

Clare were not so easily satisfied. At the further end of the long room, where their whispers could not reach Mrs. Courtly, they lay back on a settee, the shaded lamp-light defining dimly the silhouette of their two heads, and touching more sharply the edges of the girl's pink and silver dress, and the tips of patent-leather which terminated the man's long legs, crossed one over the other. That was the picture which often rose before Grace's eyes, when she pondered on what her brother's fate would be. The actual dialogue would not have struck an eavesdropper as sentimental. But then there are so many different avenues to the citadel of the affections.

She was fond of referring to England. "Have you ever stayed at Lord Grantham's?"

"No. He never asked me, and I shouldn't have gone if he had."

"Why not?"

"Oh! I don't know. He's not in my set. I shouldn't meet anyone I knew there."

"That is very civil to me! We stayed there quite a number of times. Pray, why is he not in 'your set'? Is he not of as good a family as there is in England?"

"Yes. It's a very old title. But rank isn't everything. That is a mistake Americans are so apt to make. Men of rank are not always much thought of in society."

"Well I don't care whether he is much thought of or not, *I* think he is a very nice fellow."

"If I had known he was such a great friend of yours, I wouldn't have said a word. You asked me."

She laughed, "How funny Englishmen are! I see I must never ask one man his opinion of another, unless he belongs to the same club—if I don't mean him to be sniffed at. Well! I am never influenced by anyone's opinion. If I like people, I like them, and if I don't, I don't."

"Capital! You have the courage of your opinions. So few girls have the pluck to do that, to stick to what they think. I wonder if you will always remain like that."

She was playing with her fan, and looked up, to find his eyes fixed upon her. She laughed lightly.

"I have been chaffed pretty badly about being an Anglo-maniac since I returned home;

but I don't mind. I like England and English men. I don't care so much about English women. They are kind of condescending, I find, and I suspect they are a little jealous of us; so many of our girls having carried off their young men. In short, I believe our best time with you is over."

"Why do you say that? I thought people were so very civil to you?"

"So they were—many of them—more than civil; but my eyes and ears were wide open. I saw things—I heard things said about me; and I know we were refused invitations to several balls—because we were American."

"No, only because society is already much too big for our small houses; and as to jealousy, isn't that a feminine form of appreciation?"

"Do males rise superior to it?"

They both laughed.

On the Monday morning, Barham returned early to Cambridge, and Ferrars had the field once again to himself.

Soon after breakfast a buggy came round, drawn by a famous American trotter, who had won several matches, and who, to the uninitiated, was as ugly a specimen of the equine race as could well be seen. His long straight neck, poked forward, his flat back, and his action in walking or ambling, were utterly opposed to the Greek, or even the mediæval, conception of what a horse should be, and how he should move. It appeared, moreover, that this wonderful pace which was the animal's *specialité*, could not be maintained for more than a mile or so. Therefore, for all practical purposes, it seemed a useless gift, purchased at the sacrifice of grace and beauty; but perhaps Grace was the only one present who thought this. Mordaunt, for whose special delectation the buggy was brought, was invited by Mrs. Courtly to take Miss Planter for a drive. Of course he was delighted; the girl did not hesitate; only Mrs. Planter thought fit to say to Grace, —

"We should not do this in England, of course, but here in the country, you know, and especially in the west where we live, the young people drive out together, all the time."

"If it is the custom, why not?"

"I was afraid you might think it sort of strange. But I assure you Clare has been *very* strictly brought up."

Mordaunt's declaration on his return was that he had never enjoyed a drive so much in his life, and his untiring attendance upon Clare during the remainder of the day first made Grace think seriously of his condition. She lay awake some time that night, and her meditations ended in a resolve to speak to Mrs. Courtly. It was curious that hitherto she had not found an opportunity of being alone with her hostess for half an hour. Yet there was another subject on which she desired to sound her. But Mrs. Courtly seemed to live in a round of small excitement, constant and varied occupation, the preparation or execution of schemes for the pleasure of herself and others, or the benefit of others only. When driving, or walking, or sitting over the fire, she expected some of her men friends to talk to her, just as she held it imperative that some of them should be devoted to her women guests. She had no idea of allowing men to talk together, or of encouraging women to gossip with each other, when the opposite sexes met. And when did they not meet in her house?

On Tuesday morning a telegram from Mrs. Frampton, which had been delayed two days in consequence of misdirection, announced that she was on the eve of embarkation at Liverpool. As the telegram was dated the previous Saturday, she might be expected in New York the following Friday, and Mordaunt would of course go and meet her. He and Clare would therefore be but two days more under the same roof. Would this precipitate matters? or would it be the simple termination of a pastime on both sides?

Grace laid her hand on Mrs. Courtly's arm, as they were leaving the dining-room.

"May I come to your boudoir for a few minutes?"

"Why, of course!" and she led the way to that sanctuary of religion and the fine arts, defiled only in one corner by account-books, business letters, and bills of fare.

"I want to ask you a straighforward question," began Grace, plunging boldly into the subject uppermost in her thoughts, without circumlocution. "Is Miss Planter a coquette? Is she trifling with my brother, or do you think she cares the least about him?"

Mrs. Courtly smiled one of her sweet enigmatical smiles.

"My dear Miss Ballinger, is Sir Mordaunt trifling with Clare?"

Grace coloured.

"You are quite justified in returning my question. I do not believe he is. If they are thrown much more together, I believe he will be rendered very unhappy, should it prove that she cares nothing about him."

"He tells me he must go to New York by the night mail on Thursday."

"Yes, but we are going west after that, and so are the Planters. If I had an inkling of the girl's real character, I might either help him, or save him a great deal of pain."

"Clare Planter is a curious girl—in fact she is an American product, and not like any English girl. It is impossible to tell what she will do. Even her own mother does not know. I know *she* would be quite in your brother's favour, but that would have no weight with Clare, any more than opposition would have. She will probably take a long time to make up her mind as to the man she wishes to marry, but when it is once made up, nothing will change her."

"I like that. I could not wish a better

answer to my question. So then," she added laughing, "this desperate flirtation is based, on her part, upon the profoundest principles, and a sense of the importance of knowing a man well before you consent to marry him? Well, I can't disapprove of that—only the man, you see, may suffer in the process."

"Men don't suffer as we do, my dear." She gave a half-suppressed sigh. "At all events, it is never any use interfering in these matters."

"Certainly. If both are bent on this, I would be the last to interfere. But if I thought the girl were leading him on to propose, in order that she may refuse him, I would do all I could, with my aunt's help—she has immense influence with Mordaunt—to save him from a Will-o'-the-Wisp dance half over America."

"If I understand Clare—which I don't feel certain I do—she will never be the slave of her senses. Flirtation does not affect her in *that* way; she will never be precipitated into an engagement. She is capable of strong attachment; but that is a plant of slow growth. She is genuinely attached to her father. If she marries an Englishman, she will never consent to be as much separated from her parents and her country as so many American women are."

"I am glad of that. Though I confess I think Mrs. Planter a bore, I shouldn't wish her daughter to think so. If you are right, the girl has a great deal of character, and though I see her faults—which are partly those of training and association—I believe her good qualities would preponderate with me in the long run."

"I think they would. She has a rare power—rare even for an American—of adapting herself to the country, the people, the circumstances, which surround her. If she were stuck down in a ranche in Texas, without a 'help,' I believe she would make the beds and cook the dinner as well as anyone—"

"Splendid!" cried Grace, enthusiastically. "I thought her adaptability might be limited to catching the tone of society. I am glad it has a wider range. I begin to hope now that our parting on Thursday may not be final."

"But *you* are not going on Thursday? You stay on with me, I hope, and meet your brother in Boston, when he brings your aunt there."

"Thank you so much, but I have written to Mrs. Barham, to ask if she likes to receive me for a day or two."

Mrs. Courtly opened her eyes. "I suppose you know it is only a very small rectory? I hope you will be comfortable."

"Oh! I am not afraid of that."

"Well, I shall meet you in Boston. I will go to the 'Vendôme' for a few days—I often do so—in order to present you to some of my friends. You should see something of its society, while there. But I am so sorry you won't stay longer with me." Then she added in a low voice, "Quintin Ferrars will be in despair. He has so few friends."

"Yes," said Grace, slowly. "That is a pity, and I am sure it is his own fault. Will you tell me something of his past life? I am interested in him, otherwise I suppose I should not care what his past had been. He puzzles me. I feel there is something to be explained, he is so very odd. But I have not *le mot de l'énigme.*"

"No one here knows it, but it is quite right *you* should. I meant to have told you before. He married a Spanish woman many years ago, a widow. She was a beautiful creature, I am told, and she had an ample fortune, but she turned out to be thoroughly bad. He left her after a few months, and has never seen her since. She returned to the name of her first husband, and washed her hands of Quintin. He never took a farthing of her money, which she has spent chiefly, they say, on Prince Lamperti—"

"Prince Lamperti! Do you mean that that woman, Madame Moretto, is Mr. Ferrars' wife?"

"Yes, that was her first husband's name."

"Good heavens! that explains his strange conduct in New York. He must have seen his wife, once when he left us suddenly, and another time I remember his going out of the room abruptly when the Princess Lamperti entered it. But, he is divorced, I suppose?"

"No, not yet. I will tell you the whole story. Very few people knew of his marriage; he has no near relations. He was married abroad, and during the short time he and his wife were together, he never came to America. When he learnt what she was, he was so disgusted and ashamed, that, as she chose to return to her first husband's name, he thought it useless to have the scandal of a divorce. He felt sure he should never wish to marry again, himself—he thinks differently now—and so he tried to forget that terrible episode, though it had left him bruised and embittered, to a degree no one who did not know him before, can imagine. Lately, the Princess Lamperti, finding it impossible to reclaim her husband, at last decided to divorce him. Whereupon Madame Moretto resolved to come over here, and live in the State of Rhode Island for six months, in order to sue for *her* divorce, on the plea of her husband's desertion, and want of ' maintenance,' though, as she is a rich woman, and he comparatively a poor man, that is absurd. But Quintin, of course, did not oppose it ; and now he is very, *very* glad. He would have gone on, a miserable, lonely man, to the end of his life, I suppose, if she had not moved in the matter. I hope now, he may find consolation and happiness in the course of time."

"He is certainly much to be pitied," said Grace, a little drily, as it seemed to Mrs. Courtly, " most of all, I think, because his troubles seem to have destroyed his belief in all goodness."

"No, not *all* goodness; only the greater part of what passes as such. I assure you he never doubts yours."

"I had rather he believed in humanity, generally, than in me, whom I suspect he understands very little."

And then Grace turned the subject, and shortly afterwards left the room.

CHAPTER II.

The reply to Grace's note, which Mrs. Barham wired back, was to the effect that the Rev. James Barham and she would be delighted to receive Miss Ballinger at Fellbridge on Thursday, for as long as she could find it convenient to remain with them. It was arranged, therefore, that Mordaunt should telegraph to his sister on Mrs. Frampton's arrival, and that they should meet at the Brunswick Hotel in Boston, whichever day her aunt liked to leave New York.

Tuesday and Wednesday passed without event or conversation worth record. Mr. Laffon and Burton had departed; other visitors came and went, some for the afternoon, some to dine and sleep. Mrs. Courtly's hospitality was great; but she did not resemble the man in the parable, who thought any company was better than none. She was seldom alone, and people of all kinds, and all tastes, met in her house; but they must have something to recommend them, they must bring some gryst to the mill of society. One night they danced; some boys from Harvard and some girls from Boston having arrived; and to see Mrs. Courtly's light, graceful figure flying round with a beardless youth, was really a pretty sight, and did not appear incongruous.

> "Age cannot wither her, nor custom stale
> Her infinite variety,"

murmured Quintin Ferrars, as he watched her.

"Yes," Grace replied, "I never knew so many-sided a human being. Nothing seems to come amiss to her—except unkindness." She had grown really fond of her hostess, though two characters more opposed it would have been hard to find.

Since Paul Barham's departure, Ferrars had found many opportunities of being alone with Grace, and, even after Mrs. Courtly's revelations, she did not avoid these, for, as she said truly, she was interested in the man, and she pitied him doubly since she knew his story.

She did not respect or admire him; but he was clever, and her very outspoken criticism of his opinions not being taken amiss, it was just possible she might exercise some beneficial influence over him. So he had himself declared, and what woman is there who would refuse to believe such a declaration? After Thursday they might probably never meet again. If she could do him any good, if any words of hers could alter the current of this unhappy man's feelings towards his fellow-men, she must spare no pains during the short time that was left her to effect this.

So when, on that Thursday morning, he asked her to take a last walk with him, she would not refuse. Overhead was a hard, blue sky, like a stone, with yet harder white clouds driven across it by a bitter north-east wind. The shrubs were bowed earthwards; the brown last year's leaves from the garden, the pulverized stone-dust from the road, were swept along till they found refuge in some corner where their relentless driver could no longer flog them.

Grace, clad in her ulster and stalking-cap, did not fear the wind, but as it rendered talking difficult, she proposed that they should seek the shelter of the fir-wood. There, the turbulence of the wind was only heard in the upper branches, a great quiet reigned over the soft, tawny soil, carpeted with pine-needles, upon which their footsteps fell.

His beginning was not happy.

"Why are you going away? Why do you go and stay with these Barhams, a country minister and his wife, with whom I am sure you can have nothing in common?"

"I like Mrs. Barham and her son very much—that is why I go."

"You will turn that conceited young fellow's head." Then he added suddenly, without looking at her, "You are the only woman I ever met who seems to have no idea of her own power."

She remained silent for a moment, then said slowly, "I have not found it so. My life has rather shown me that I have very little."

"With certain people you can do anything you choose," he persisted, "but that is not my point. Of course many women have that power, for good or ill. My point is that you don't know when you have it—you don't see the tremendous influence you may exercise upon some lives—upon mine, for instance. You may change all my views of life, turn curses into blessings, misery into joy, and you do not see it!"

She was startled; for the first time the truth flashed upon her mind. It was impossible to misunderstand the meaning of those words. This man, in whom she had taken a purely impersonal intellectual interest, whom she had never led by word, or look, or action, to make love to her, this man with a wife living, from whom he was not yet divorced, dared ′to suggest to her the hopes he entertained. A flush of indignation suffused her face. She felt angry with him, and doubly angry with herself for her stupidity.

"You are quite right. *I did not see*, and I do not choose to see now," she said at last. "I told Mrs. Courtly yesterday, that you understood me very little; this proves it."

"Why? Is it an offence to say this?"

"It should be so. But let that pass. I repeat that you understand me very little, since you seem to have mistaken the nature of my friendly feeling towards you. I am very sorry if—"

"No, no—don't say you are sorry . . . I have been precipitate, I know. . . . We are going to part now—and I felt I must speak —that I must tell you how different life has appeared to me since I came to know you well. I have never felt for any woman what I feel for you—"

"You should not say that," she interrupted quickly. "It is enough that I know your story."

"And have you no pity for me, then? Can you not see how the great deception of my life turned all my feelings into gall, until I met you? Can you not understand my anxiety *now* for freedom—freedom, which I shall obtain in less than six months? Will you not—"

"Stay! Mr. Ferrars. Situated as you are, it is hardly showing much respect for me to use this language. But no matter. Understand me, once for all. If you were fifty times free, it would make no difference in my feeling towards you. I am sorry you have disturbed the pleasant terms on which we were."

"Will you hold out no hope? No possibility in the future?" he asked, in a low, husky voice.

She shook her head. "None, Mr. Ferrars; none."

"Fool!" he muttered; and in his sudden passion he broke the stick in his hand. "Why did I speak? Not from want of respect for you, believe me, but because we were going to part, and I resolved never to follow you— never to persecute you with my presence—unless I had a ray of hope. Just one ray was all I wanted. God! If you knew what it was to be utterly alone in the world, without a creature you care for, or who cares for you!" He flung the two pieces of stick among the trees. "That is all my life is worth now. I was insane enough to fancy it might begin again. That dream is ended. You will forgive me— won't you?"

She made no reply. Platitudes, good advice were worse than useless at such a moment. Her transient indignation had given place to real sorrow for the man; but to express this would only add fuel to the fire. They had reached a point in the wood where two paths met. At the further end of one she saw Mordaunt and Miss Planter. Their backs were towards her; they were in deep conversation, as they slowly paced along. Grace naturally chose the other path, and it was that which led back to the house. When they were yet some yards distant, she said,—

"Let all this be forgotten between us, we have both made a mistake. But I hope, by-and-by, if we should meet again, that you will let me feel the same friendly regard for you that I did before—before you allowed yourself to speak to me of this foolish fancy, which I am sure will pass away."

"Never," he said in a hoarse voice, "it will never *pass away*—but I promise—I swear to you that you shall not be troubled with this madness of mine again. Let us part here—I can't face all those people—God bless you! You are the best woman I have ever known, and for your sake I shall think better of humanity henceforward."

He wrung her hand; and his face was deadly white, as he turned to enter the house by a side door. An hour later he was gone. No one but Mrs. Courtly saw him; and that discreet friend announced at luncheon that Quintin Ferrars had been called suddenly and unexpectedly away.

In the meantime the other two had been walking in the fir-wood for the best part of an hour. If we take up their dialogue during the last ten minutes, we shall sufficiently understand what preceded it.

"You say you like no one else? That there is no other fellow you'd sooner marry?"

"No, there is none; I like you better than Lord Grantham, though I really liked him very much, and better than any one else who has proposed to me in London or New York. I like you awfully, I really *do*. But to marry— Oh! I think a man takes a deal of knowing, before one can make up one's mind to marry him."

"Haven't we had exceptional opportunities here of knowing each other? Far better, I'm sure, than if we had spent a season in London, or a winter in New York together! I feel I know your bright, sweet nature thoroughly, and—"

"Oh! but you don't. I am ever so full of contradictions. As fast as ever you get hold of one thing, you'll find there's something else quite contrary. I wish a thing, and I don't wish it. Sometimes I fancy I should like to marry an Englishman, and then again I think I should prefer living in my own country. I am not sure about anything, you see, yet, and therefore I mean to go around, for quite a time, and feel certain before I settle."

"I want you to feel certain. But if in six months you don't change your mind—"

"But I have not made up my mind! If I had, I should not feel like changing it in six months. I am changeable now, but I don't mean to be so, by-and-by. When I was in England, of course I had quite a number of proposals; but, except for Lord Grantham— I think he really *did* like me—I felt pretty sure they only wanted to marry me, because they heard pa-pa was rich, and I was his only child, and that wasn't good enough for *me*."

"I should think not! I'd marry you gladly if you hadn't a penny—try me. Tell your father not to settle a dollar on you. Men in business, Americans especially, I believe, are not fond of making settlements. I'm not rich, but I've quite enough for us to live on."

"Oh! that is not it. I think I can tell when a man is pretending. And I am sure you are not pretending. All the same," she added with an arch smile, " I expect your heart would recover, if you were told you were never to see me again, though you might feel pretty badly at first."

"I don't say it wouldn't," returned Mordaunt, quick enough to see that frankness was his best policy. " I'm not going to tell a lot of humbug about my heart being broken, which you wouldn't believe. Of course I have flirted a good deal. A guardsman of eight-and-twenty must have had some affairs. You wouldn't believe me if I said I hadn't. But I have never been hard hit till now. I am honestly and heartily in love with you. I think you are the dearest girl in the world, and I shall go on persevering as long as I see you don't prefer another fellow. If you *do*, I shall be awfully cut up, though I shall try and prevent the world's seeing it; and, I suppose, in the course of time, I shall marry someone else who throws her cap at me. She'll have to make the running. I shan't be a bit in love."

" Mam-ma says love is not necessary at first — that it grows and strengthens after marriage — that violent fancies are seldom lasting."

"You run no danger of that kind, apparently," was his reproachful reply. "You speak as if you had no heart."

"I don't know if I have one or not. If I was sure I had, I would marry the man right away who made me sure. And when I feel sure I have *not*, I shall marry—well, I suppose anyone."

"For ambition?"

"Perhaps."

There was a long silence. Irrepressible, "bumptious," as he was often called, Mordaunt Ballinger on this occasion was reduced to silence. His eyes bent upon the ground, his hands thrust deep into the pockets of his ulster, he kicked the fir-cones with his yellow leather boots, as they paced the wood, while the girl, erect, keen-sighted, with a brilliant colour on her fair cheek, glanced at him from time to time, and then away through the red-stemmed pines to where the blue smoke curled up from the chimneys of the house.

It was she who spoke first.

"Where are you going after Boston?"

"To Colorado. And you? Do you remain at Pittsburg till the spring?"

"I think not. It doesn't agree with mam-ma. Perhaps we may go to the Pacific Slope."

"Where is that? Don't laugh. Do you mean California?"

"Why, of course. Don't the hills slope down to the Pacific?"

"And where do you stop there?"

"Possibly at Monterey; just the loveliest place in the whole world, I believe."

"I think we might come, too. I didn't mean to go so far, but if—if you—would like—"

"Like? Why, of course I should! It would be just delightful. We would have a real good time, wandering by that lovely shore, watching the seals, and driving through the cypress forest. I shall expect to meet you there."

"Then I shall come."

That afternoon the brother and sister parted at the Boston Railway Station, when Mordaunt saw his sister and her maid into a train which would deposit them in half an hour at Fellbridge, the small town of which the Rev. Joseph Barham was the rector.

But little had passed between Grace and Mordaunt. Clare Planter's name had not been mentioned. The two girls had parted with cordiality, when Clare had said, " I hope we may meet in California. Your brother says we shall."

" Indeed ?" Grace replied. " I did not know he meant to go as far." Then she added with emphasis, " If *you* wish it, I hope we may."

She sought no explanation from Mordaunt ; she respected his reticence, understood his rather forced hilarity at moments, and then his long lapses into silence. It was better so ; she did not much believe in confidences.

Mr. Barham met his English visitor at the Fellbridge Station, and while her maid waited to accompany the porter who was to wheel her box on a truck down the street, the minister conducted Grace to the rectory.

He was a tall, handsome man of five-and-forty, with hair still untouched with grey, which may have helped to make a middle-aged face, in which high cheek-bones and a prominent chin were the chief defects, look somewhat hard. The silver that years scatters on our head is a wondrous softener; as silver, in life, is so often found to be.

He greeted the young Englishwoman with a grave, old-fashioned courtesy to which she was unaccustomed.

"This visit is a pleasure to which Mrs. Barham has been looking forward for several weeks, Miss Ballinger. You will take us as we are, simple folk, living in a simple way. You can have expected nothing else in coming to a minister's house, so I make no apologies. We will make you as comfortable as we can, and show you what little there is to see in our neighbourhood."

They stopped before a green-painted wooden house, in no way dissimilar from its fellows in the long, wide street. It stood in a "yard," perhaps a quarter of an acre square, with half a dozen stripling trees, and a bush or two, irregularly dispersed round it. Fence or paling there was none, dividing it from the road, or from its neighbours. It had a "piazza," or covered balcony running along the front, in which grew two shrubs in pots, but there was no border or bed of brown frozen earth, telling of a past-summer's garden. The exterior was certainly discouraging.

Mrs. Barham, who had been watching at the window for them, came to the door herself, but not before it had been opened by an Irish parlour-maid, with an aroma of Tipperary still hanging about her. Her very hair seemed to have a brogue. But behind her shone the sweet, glad face of Saul's mother, and the two delicate hands which Grace declared she would have recognized anywhere, were extended to greet her.

The interior of the house presented some pleasant features, indicative of work and home life. On this account it seemed to Grace more cheerful than many of the sumptuous dwellings she had visited in New York. The "parlour" had books on one table, Mrs. Barham's work-basket on another, her writing materials, and letters on a third. There was no open fire-place, and the heat from the stove struck Grace as oppressive, coming from the sharp air of the February afternoon. But she was beginning to get acclimatized to the atmosphere of American hotels, railway-cars, and most private houses, Brackley being an exception.

She threw open her fur jacket as she sat down.

"How nice it is to see you again—and to be under your roof!" she exclaimed.

"It was lovely of you to offer yourself, Miss Ballinger. . . . I am afraid you find the room too warm? Won't you take your jacket right off?" Then calling, "Molly! you might bring the tea, and—Molly! some blueberry jam, if you please, and the Boston crackers. Joseph—" this to her husband, who, divested of his great-coat and over-shoes, now entered the parlour—an honour he rarely paid that apartment till the evening—"I hope you feel like coming to sit down here, and having a quiet cup of tea with us? He does work so hard, Miss Ballinger. I am so glad to get him away from his study and his parish-work for half an hour."

Mr. Barham did not reply to this. He sat down stiffly, crossed his legs, and said,—

"We expect our son presently."

"You saw him on Sunday?" asked Mrs. Barham, anxiously. "Did you think him looking ill?"

"Hardly as well as on board ship—but that was natural."

"His heart is in his work, and he works too hard," sighed the mother.

"He does his duty. He can do no less. You observe that Mrs. Barham has 'work' on the brain," said the father, with just so much upward inclination of the curves of the mouth as might, by courtesy, be called a smile. "That which a man's hand finds to do, should be done with all his might. I should regret if a son of mine thought otherwise."

"Ah, Joseph, but with Saul you know very well that though the spirit is willing, the flesh is weak."

"Saul is free to do as he will. I do not coerce him. He has an independence. He may travel on the continent of Europe till he is strong—and you may go with him. I have told you so both, quite a number of times, but he prefers to work at home, and now that he has gotten this professorship, I guess it will be hard to induce him to give it up. He has the grit of a true American, Miss Ballinger. He won't cave in till he is forced."

"Then I hope you will force him—if his health suffers."

"Thank you for saying that," said Mrs.

Barham, eagerly. "My husband is just as anxious as I am about our son, but he won't speak. He says a man must work out the problem of life for himself. I say we old ones should help the young with our experience."

Molly here entered, staggering under a tea-tray, laden with buckwheat and corn cakes. She set it down, sweeping to right and left the books on the table; then, with a mighty sigh, which seemed as though it would burst every button in her bodice, she placed her arms akimbo, and stood there awaiting further instructions.

"You might bring some milk, Molly," observed Mrs. Barham, in mild remonstrance. Then, lifting the lid of the teapot, "are you sure the water boiled?"

"Faith, m'm, I thought ye wanted your tray in a hurry, and for once it didn't mather."

A distressed look came over her mistress's face. "It always *must* boil, Molly. I have told you so before. Could not the cook have put it on the fire sooner?"

"She and me was helpin' Pat Malone wid the lady's box, which was that big we had the divil's own work to get it upstairs, m'm."

"Do not speak of the devil's work in that light way," said her master sternly.

"I wasn't manein' to shpake of him in a light way, sorr, for indade it was mighty heavy, and—"

"Well!" interrupted her mistress, quickly. "You might run and make some fresh tea—for this is hardly warm; and mind the water *boils* this time." Having thus got rid of the irrepressible Hibernian housemaid, Mrs. Barham turned to her guest, with a piteous smile. "These helps are our greatest trial. They come over here raw—very raw—material. If one gets an honest girl like this, one must put up with her faults. One dare not get rid of her, for fear of getting something worse."

The shrill whistle of a steam-engine was now heard, not far distant.

"That is the train from Cambridge," said Saul's mother.

CHAPTER III.

OF the quartette that sat down to dinner that evening—a homely dinner, without pretension—three at least were in the best of spirits, and ready to laugh over Molly's peculiar methods of service. Mr. Barham had little sense of humour; in that respect, at least, he was not American; he took life very gravely. It needed all his son's fire to keep things alight in so damp an atmosphere. But Saul's cheek was flushed; he was voluble, excited. Grace had never seen him so brilliant, so evidently happy, and at his ease. For here he was at home, with no carping listeners; he could give his fun and fancy play, and this was the occasion which he had thought of so often, and which he had desired so keenly to bring about, during the past two months. It was not in his father's power to depress him to-night. Had he not that gracious delightful creature opposite, all to himself? No Jem Gunning beside her, as at the *Teutonic* board, nor cynic Ferrars, as at Brackley. His empire for a few brief hours at least was undivided.

Molly having heaved a joint down before the master, whispered very audibly to the mistress,—

" Will ye be doin' y'r own stretchin', m'm, for a few minutes, whiles I fetch the praties, and squob pie ? "

Grace made as though she heard not, but Saul laughed outright, as the girl scuttled from the room.

" You have no idea, Miss Ballinger, what Molly is, until you have seen her in the presence of an Irish patriot. We had one here last week. I may as well own to you,"—here he gave a droll glance at the minister, whose stern glance was riveted on the joint, which he was endeavouring to penetrate with a plated knife.[1]

—" I may as well own to you that my father has Home Rule proclivities. So he offered Mr. ——— hospitality, when he and his colleagues were down here, on their Propa-

---

[1] Economy of labour has almost abolished the use of steel knives throughout the United States.

ganda tour, last week. Molly outdid herself on that occasion."

"I can believe it," laughed Grace, "from what she said to me."

"What she said to you?" cried Mrs. Barham. "Why, when?"

Before dinner. I found her haranguing my maid upon the wrongs of 'ould Ireland,' and upon the privilege I enjoyed of sleeping in the bed which had been occupied by 'the biggest Irish pathriot, barrin' Misther Parnell,' a few days ago. When I entered, she continued in the same strain, and assured me, 'there is nothin' changed but the sheets, since the blessed man lay here—and sure y'r dreams will be all the sweeter, miss, for knowin' it.'"

Mrs. Barham and Saul laughed heartily; Mr. Barham alone was silent. When he spoke, it was to say gravely,—

"One cannot expect English persons to feel as we do on this subject. Few take a dispassionate view of questions that touch their own interests."

"Very few," said his son, smiling. "You were a strong abolitionist, because you were a

Northerner, and did not possess slaves. Rives from New Orleans, who is ruined, swears the coloured people were far happier, more prosperous, better educated and cared for, in a state of slavery than they now are. It all depends, as you say, on the point of view."

"I am no politician," said Grace, "but I was in Ireland five years ago, and again last year, and I was struck with the improved aspect of the people, of the land, of everything since Mr. Balfour's reign. That is the only 'point of view' *I* have, but I daresay I am quite wrong. Women have capital instincts—I think my own instincts about people are almost unerring; but my opinions on other subjects are generally worth nothing. My aunt always says so."

"That is, no doubt, when they differ from hers," observed Saul, with a smile.

"My aunt is a very clever woman, with decided views about everything in Heaven above and in the earth beneath. She cannot tolerate compromise, or shilly-shallying, or weakness of any kind. She often upbraids me for not disliking people more cordially than I do. If I don't like them, they are indifferent to me. So few seem worth hating—at least judged by the aspect they present to the world. Of course, one *may* entertain murderers, as well as angels, unawares."

"You hated Lady Clydesdale, I think—just a *little ?* I hear she is in Boston."

"I hope I shan't meet her. Is she popular there ?"

"She is a clever woman in her way, and holds the same views that some of our advanced women do—only samer. Then she is a countess."

Here he smiled.

"Well, now, you have an English countess coming with the most democratic and subversive ideas among us staunch Republicans. You must confess there is something fascinating about it."

"I can't say, not being a Republican. I only know *she* is not fascinating. Her manners are odious, and then she has a most uncharitable tongue. She is just the sort of woman to give the worst impression of an English lady to foreigners."

"Do you call us foreigners ?"

She laughed.

"What do you call yourselves ? I am quite ready to accept your own definition."

"We call ourselves your sixth cousins—once removed."

"Very well; then you must not expect the privileges that attach to aliens."

"What are they? I never heard of them."

"Oh! it is a small matter, but one which some of your countrymen cavil at—the question of precedence. If we treat them as of our own family, and follow our own laws of etiquette, I have heard them say it was discourteous."

"Then they were fools—*non raggionam' di lor*. Republicans should be above such rubbish as that."

"The first shall be last, and the last shall be first!" said his father, looking up from the havoc of meat before him.

The conversation was carried on chiefly between Saul and Grace. Mrs. Barham occasionally put in her oar, a gentle tentative stroke, never out of time, never impeding progress; but the main work was in the hands of the two strong young pullers. The minister said but little. The talk was of things concerning which he knew nothing, or the echo of which, at most, had reached him from a distance, without awakening much interest. In his narrow sphere, where there was no circulating library, and where he rarely came in contact with a mind which had left the beaten highroads, along which its possessor jogged contented daily to his business, or his farm, the air was exhausted, vitiated. There was no free current of thought as in more spacious centres of activity, where men meet, discuss, and learn the lessons that are taught by friction. Not that the village was a dream of idylic peace, or free from the jealousies that are born of theological controversy. How could it be otherwise, in a comparatively small community, which boasted, besides the Episcopal Church, of an Unitarian, a Baptist, a first Methodist, a second Methodist, and a Congregational Chapel? It was astonishing that they all fared as well together as they did; but in the nature of things, discussion and criticism constantly arose, and it was Mr. Barham's misfortune that these conflicts of opinion never tended to enlarge his own strongly fortified views. For the minds with which he had to deal were all distinctly inferior to his own. Endowed with considerable capacity, combative, obstinate, and unswerving in rectitude and his idea of duty he might, under different circumstances, have become a modern St. Paul. At least so his son said. But then St. Paul had been, as we know, buffeted about a good deal, in the course of which process he had learned a considerable knowledge of the world. It is true that, like St. Paul, Mr. Barham was neither diffident nor humble. It was possible to conceive that he might, at the close of his life, say, " I have fought a good fight, I have kept the faith. Henceforth there is laid up for me a crown of righteousness." But he never could have written, " I am made all things to all men," for a more uncompromising opponent in discussion, or one who less understood the wisdom of yielding in small things, never stepped the earth.

Between Saul and his father there were differences of opinion on other subjects than that of Home Rule; but the son, while he had inherited some of Mr. Barham's obstinacy and tenacity of purpose, had a more plastic mind, and possessed the invaluable capacity of being able to hold his tongue. Thus he never argued with his father; knowing that it would be useless to assail the bulwarks behind which his opinions were entrenched; and doubly reluctant, now that he had left home, to enter into controversy which might leave some soreness of feeling behind it. The father respected his son: his character, his attainments, the estimation in which he knew Saul was held. Therein lay the young man's strength. But for this, it could hardly have been that altercation should not have arisen, from time to time, between a man of so dominant a disposition as Mr. Barham, and the one human being who had grown up under his direct influence, and upon whom it might be expected he would have imposed his views. A little gentle banter, as on this occasion, was all that the young professor ever permitted himself towards his father; and this the minister received much as a majestic Newfoundland does the bark of a puppy. It was beneath his notice.

"My father, you see, has become a total abstainer lately," he said to Grace towards the end of dinner, "and it is no use my mother's quoting St. Paul to him—'Drink no longer water, but use a little wine for thy stomach's sake.' The pitchers of iced water he consumes in a day, would float a lugger. I have remarked to him occasionally that excesses in iced water are as pernicious—or perhaps more so—than in spirits ; but my words of wisdom fall on inattentive ears."

Grace replied, "All I know is we were specially warned against falling into the habit, when we came to America. As to my aunt, she thinks there are 'germs' or 'microbes,' or something, in every glass, and would sooner die of thirst, I believe, than drink water which she could not trace to its very source."

Even the minister himself smiled at this; but he did not attempt to argue the point, it was not worth while. His attitude throughout the evening was the same; that of a listener, standing somewhat aloof from the subjects discussed; rarely a participator in the discussion. The ground they traversed was never personal. Grace felt that her curiosity about the young professor's views and aspirations must be curbed in the presence of his father, before whom she instinctively knew he would not speak openly.

The next morning Saul returned to his work, and Mrs. Barham proposed taking Grace to visit that magnificent female University, "The

Wellesley College," which was only a short distance by rail. It far surpasses, in extent and scope, as Grace found, any similar institution in England. Seven hundred girls were receiving instruction from the very best professors in classics, modern languages, literature, science, and art, according to their proclivities, and the object each had in view. The main building, and the fine park in which it stands, were the donation of a man who lost his only child, and devoted his vast fortune to the erection and endowment of this college. For sixty pounds yearly, a girl has every privilege belonging to it—including bed and board; and the education of the body is no less well cared for than that of the mind. There is a gymnasium and a big lake, where the girls row in summer time, and skate in winter. They looked blooming and merry, this bright February morning, flying over the ice, their young voices, pitched in a high key, rippling along the sharpened air, as they pursued each other.

Their English visitor was exceedingly interested. The aspect of the place and of the students alike charmed her; it was so cheerful, so far removed from the sternness of the Academic Grove. Here each girl seemed to be pursuing with enthusiasm, and with a joyousness of spirit which struck Grace as wholly un-English, the studies she had selected as likely to be most serviceable to her in after life. There was no enforced "curriculum," no obligatory course of learning. A high standard of excellence in each department stimulated the energies and the ambition of the students; it seemed in no instance to have crushed them. The common objection made to women taking up serious studies, that it unfits them for domestic life, and in many instances frightens away the would-be suitor, was effectually answered when Grace was told that nearly every girl who had taken a high degree, and had left the college meaning to earn her livelihood by mental labour, had married within a few months, and had settled down, contented in the home that had been offered her.

"Are all these girls of one class?" asked Grace, of Mrs. Barham.

"No; some are the daughters of rich men, who have no need to work for their living. The greatest proportion, of course, mean to become governesses, for whom there is a great and constantly-increasing demand. Some again, will become doctors, some designers, and so on. Quite a number become writers for the periodicals or for the daily press."

" Oh ! I hope they don't become interviewers, like that dreadful Miss Clutch, who forced herself on me in New York ? "

" Why, no, I should think not, for their refining education must render such a course most repulsive. But then, all interviewers are not like Miss Clutch, you must not think it. Some of them are quite ladies, who would never force themselves on anyone."

" Who was the visitor with a charming face, whom you introduced to me as Miss Forster ? "

" She is quite a friend of mine, though we do not often meet, who is greatly interested in the college, and visits there every week. It is an object, you see, for a woman who is alone in the world. I often think what I should do without my husband and my son."

" Alone in the world ! " That was what Quintin Ferrars had called himself. It was the second time within a few days, that the phrase had forced itself upon her, and this time it struck her, like a blow. Would not she be "alone in the world," when Mordy had taken unto himself a wife, and no longer needed her? She would never marry for expediency's sake, or for any reason but one. Therefore, it seemed tolerably sure now, that she would be left "alone in the world." How strange, that when two people cared for each other—and she knew, no matter what she might say to Mordy, that Ivor Lawrence *did* care for her—how strange that a mistaken pride should be suffered to divide them! But, then, might there not also be mistaken pride on her part, which had held her back hitherto from writing?

As these thoughts sped through her mind, in the train, on their way back, Mrs. Barham observed the far-away look on her companion's face, and was silent. That evening, on Saul's return home to dinner, this self-communing bore unexpected fruit in the course of her conversation with the young man. They were sitting alone in the twilight; both Saul's parents being out of the room. He coughed a good deal, and looked ill, the excitement of the previous evening having passed; and, without showing the concern she felt, she questioned him as to his health and his work.

"I am afraid you take too much out of yourself."

"I can't do less," he replied. "If I was at home here, doing nothing, I should be much worse. I must have work; and my best relaxation is to discuss things with my friends, men whose ways of thought are congenial with mine. My father's, you see, are not. He is a splendid man. I admire and respect him immensely. But we both avoid discussion, knowing that neither will ever convince the other. So it would never do for me to live at home."

"I can understand that. Family controversy is always disagreeable. Have you at Harvard any friend with whom you are really intimate? any one towards whom you feel as a brother?"

"Yes, one: a man to whom I am not afraid of speaking openly on nearly every subject, feeling sure he will understand, even if he does not agree with me."

There was a pause. Grace, who rarely hesitated, hesitated now, before she said,—

"If that friend had done something which you could not understand, something which seemed incompatible with his character, and that he remained silent, that he explained nothing, what would you do? Would you write to him? or, would you rather say, 'I will not allow my trust to be shaken, because I do not understand his conduct. He has his own reasons for remaining silent. It is not for me to force an explanation from him.'"

He looked at her fixedly for a moment, then answered, in his decided way,—

"There is a higher trust than that implied by silence, the confidence that my friend will not misunderstand me. I should certainly speak. If he says, 'I can tell you nothing;' that is enough. My trust would remain unshaken; but I am bound, by that very trust, to speak openly to him, not to let the shadow of misapprehension exist between us."

"Those are brave words. I believe you are right. False pride often prevents such directness in real life, and," she added, with a smile, "still more often in novels. But, of course, there may be a complication of causes, which renders it more difficult to speak in—in some cases, than in others."

"Of course; but I fancy the difficulty

depends more upon the character of the speaker than the circumstances. You, for instance, might speak to any one whom you had really made your *friend*, without fear of misconception, no matter under what circumstances."

She looked away. "I am glad you think that. I shall remember your words."

Here Molly burst into the room, with a telegram for Grace in one hand, and a paraffin lamp, which in her haste, she nearly upset, in the other.

"The bhoy's a-waitin' for the answer, bekase it's paid for."

The telegram ran thus,—

"Aunt Susan arrived. Gone to the Hurlstones. Can meet you to-morrow in Boston, if you do not wish to stay till Monday where you are."

She wrote in pencil on the blank form,—

"Will meet you and Aunt Susan on Monday. Very happy here."

Then she handed both to the young professor.

"I am taking it for granted that your father and mother do not want to get rid of me."

"Have we not got beyond conventional

phrases? I shall not answer that, except to remind you that Sunday is the only day I can pass here. To-morrow my mother has promised to bring you over to lunch at Cambridge, where I will ask a few of our prominent men to meet you, and afterwards show you Harvard College."

That programme for the following day was carried out very satisfactorily to all concerned. The distance by steam-tram was short; the day, though intensely cold, was fine; the atmosphere, through which the brown skeletons of the trees stood up against the pale blue background, was clear. Perspectives of possible beauty when the gracious spring should clothe these skeletons with tender green, and carpet, with blade and blossom, the iron-bound earth, arose before Grace's eyes. Hitherto she had been disappointed. She had looked for bigger trees, higher hills, less tameness and monotony than she found in the New England landscape. I know not on what grounds she had built her expectations, but the reality certainly fell short of them. This short tramcar journey, however, carried her past spots of undeniable picturesqueness, where little streams, like silvery trout, twirled and darted through the red log-wood, and yellow reeds and sedges. She could conceive how pretty much of it must be in summer.

At the station of what the guide-book calls "the great academic city" Saul met them. Their walk through the main street, and villa-fringed highways to the small house where the young professor and a friend lived together, gave Grace rather the impression of a suburb; an accretion of well-to-do residences that have grown and spread out from some great centre. And though "well-to-do," those residences, as a rule, did not convey to English eyes much idea of comfort. The impossibility of any privacy in dwellings standing in "yards," unseparated from each other, and undefended even by the conventional grove of laurel, is a shock to our insular and no doubt unChristian prejudices. When Grace passed the homes of the great men whose names were "household words" to her, she marvelled, until she remembered that genius is never dependent on its surroundings.

The luncheon party was most agreeable, the five men asked to meet the ladies being not only very able in different ways, but knowing how to make their abilities serviceable to social use; as is not always the case, even with the cleverest Englishmen. After luncheon most of them had to hurry off; one, however, agreed to accompany the ladies and Saul round the University. Mrs. Barham naturally fell to him, Saul and Grace walked on in front, through the grand Memorial Hall, the University Library, the fine architectural gymnasium. Grace was properly enthusiastic.

"Harvard surpasses my expectations," she said. "I can understand your being very happy here."

"I do not think I said I was very happy," he replied. "But if I am not, the fault, no doubt, is in myself."

She looked up at him, and saw, with concern, how wan and tired he looked. He had been flushed and in brilliant spirits all the morning. He coughed at times, but then she had never known him without a cough. Now her old fear returned. But of what use was it to speak? It was clear that he would not relax in his work, still less give it up, and seek a milder climate. Like the Pompeian sentinel, he would die at his post, but never flee. Neither spoke for some minutes. Their thoughts were upon very different lines; she had forgotten his last words, and failed to see the connection of ideas, when he said,—

"I am not a philosopher, you see. I cannot accept the inevitable. When a thing is beyond a man's reach he ought not even to think about it."

"But isn't it because you do not think enough of the plain, simple thing—I would say the *duty*—that is within your reach, that you are troubled about the unattainable? Those old Romans were so wise when they said that 'a healthy mind' depended on 'a healthy body.' You ought to leave off work—I am sure you ought—and go 'right away,' as you say here, and get quite strong, before you return to this trying climate. You should do this for your mother's sake. If you resist *her* appeal, with her sweet, suffering face, of course no words of mine can be of any avail."

For a minute it seemed as though he had not heard her. His brow was knit, his lips tight clenched; he walked on without turning his head. Then, catching his breath as he spoke, he said in a low voice,—

"On the contrary. If you told me to go— to follow you—anywhere—I would do it. That is the only thing that would make me throw up my professorship."

She was painfully startled, she had not in the least anticipated this. She knew—what woman does not?—that she was admired; but their intercourse had been of such a purely friendly nature, it had never occurred to her that this young man, in whom she had not hesitated to show her deep interest, secretly nourished a far stronger feeling. They were just the same age, yet to her, in spite of his decision and force of character, he had seemed much younger. Poor fellow! Oh, the pity of it! That ill as she knew him to be, she must speak words which must wound him, words which sounded cruel even in her own ears.

"That is a responsibility I could never undertake. I can only advise you as a friend, a friend of your mother's as of yours. I can only tell you what it seems to me it is right you should do. Beyond that, I cannot direct your future."

"Of course. I never thought you would," he said in a low voice, as they entered the Memorial Hall.

His mother touched her on the shoulder at the same moment.

"Those are Lafarge's famous windows," she said. "How do you like them?"

CHAPTER IV.

SAUL did not return to Fellbridge that evening with his mother and Grace. Mrs. Barham, indeed, urged him not to do so, seeing how ill he looked; and he yielded without a word. His mother enjoined him to rest, and to go to bed early, " for you look just fairly worn out, Saul."

And when they were in the tramcar, she turned to Grace with a deep sigh, and said,—

" He has gotten back that ashy colour which he had before he went abroad. And his cough; did you hear how he coughed? Oh, Miss Ballinger, I am that down-hearted about my only boy, my only one left!"

She turned her face away, but it was not to hide any tears in her stone blue eyes. Her anxiety, her grief were far too deep for wailing.

Grace pressed silently the small gloved hand that lay on the poor mother's lap. She felt as though she were, in a measure, responsible for

Saul's condition. With a word she could send him away to some sunny clime, where he might revive, as, it seemed almost certain to her, he would not do here. But she could never speak that word.

Grace had rarely found it so hard to be cheerful as this evening. When she looked at the handsome but rigid face of her reverend host, and thought of "Little Mother" confronted by some great sorrow, with no solace but in the stern Calvinism of her husband, the girl shivered. It was probably a difficult evening to all three. The minister, who had no special anxiety about his son, exerted himself to supply the young man's place; but he felt himself to be an inefficient substitute, in conversation with his English guest. As to "Little Mother," she did her duty bravely; but it made Grace's heart ache to look into those deep, sad eyes—sad, even when the lips smiled, and she spoke lightly of indifferent matters.

When she went to her room that night, Grace sat down and wrote a letter. Its composition did not take her long; indeed, it may be said that every word of it had been burnt into her brain, many months ago. She had desired exceedingly, at that time, to write to Ivor Lawrence, and she had refrained. Again in New York, after Mordaunt had broached the subject once more, the impulse to tell the friend, who was labouring under a foul aspersion, how deeply she felt for him, had been strong. But still, moved by her brother's indignant remonstrance, she had forborne. And now, it was strange, but Saul's few words, and the reproach of her pusillanimity they carried with them, had upset all this. The forcible way in which he had confirmed her instinct—and like most women, she believed in her instincts—decided her.

This is what she wrote :—

Fellbridge, Mass., U.S.,
18th Feb., 1891.

MY DEAR MR. LAWRENCE.—I know you too well to doubt that you have some good and sufficient motive in your own eyes, for having entirely given up all communication with your friends, since this dark cloud has hung over you. That you should wilfully deprive yourself of the personal sympathy of those who would never for an instant believe you capable of a dishonourable action—no matter the amount of testimony brought against you—seems to me strange. I have waited, but waited in vain, all these months, for a line that should tell me that you trusted in my friendship; that you felt certain I could never doubt your rectitude and truth. I have been disappointed. But since it has seemed good to you to be silent, I do not see that a corresponding silence is imposed upon me; and, after some misgiving, at the risk of appearing obtrusive, I write to assure you that you have friends who watch with intense interest, but without *anxiety*, your present fight with calumny and suspicion. They never doubt but that you will come triumphantly through this ordeal. My taking up my pen to say this, may seem to you a very uncalled-for step on my part, but as I think you know me well, I am not in the least afraid of your misinterpreting it. I cannot longer allow a friend, whom I value, to suffer as I know you must be suffering, without a word to tell him of my unwavering confidence and cordial sympathy.

      Sincerely yours,
        GRACE BALLINGER.

P.S.—We are travelling in the United

States, and shall not return to England before May.

She felt more tranquil after writing this than she had done for a long time. The endeavour to put the subject away from her had failed. In the watches of the night it had come back, and upbraided her, no matter by what specious arguments she had striven to persuade herself that it was unfitting she should write. She knew her heart and intellect did not subscribe to conventional laws, though in traffic with the world her habitual conduct did so. But this was an exceptional case. Her aunt, her brother, could never understand it; because they did not understand Ivor Lawrence's peculiar character. It was that character, which, after his strange behaviour, justified this action, in her own eyes. Upon no other man could she have *forced* her sympathy. He had loved her; she felt sure of that, she could not be mistaken, and yet he had never spoken of his love. To most women this would have been a cause of misgiving, if not of offence and bitterness. It was not so to this strange girl. She felt that she could comprehend it all; the pride that kept him silent, as long as he was a poor and briefless barrister, and that shrank still further from avowal when his name was branded with infamy. But the world had not comprehended; her own kith and kin had been indignant. To one and all, the man's behaviour had seemed disgraceful. He had paid Grace such marked attention for months, as had kept other and better men aloof; then, on inheriting this vast fortune, had completely dropped her! And half this fortune must be his, it was said, even if the verdict in the approaching trial should be given against him: as an earlier will had been found, dividing Mr. Tracy's property equally between his two nephews. It was thus, as Grace knew, that her friends argued; and every effort to make them see the circumstances in a different light would be of no avail.

The next day, Sunday, Saul appeared soon after morning service. He looked as if he had not slept all night, and he coughed a great deal; but, by a resolute effort of will, he talked very much as usual. Grace should not be distressed during her last day, nor should " Little Mother," by his depression of spirits. After all, how was he worse off now, than when Grace arrived here? He knew then—he had known all along—how utterly hopeless was his attachment. He had been surprised, like a fool, into an avowal of his feelings, and he bitterly regretted it. A thin screen of ice had formed itself, since then, between him and her. Nothing, now, could melt that; but, at least, the last hours of their intercourse under his father's roof should be as little constrained as possible under the circumstances.

At parting, as he held her hand for an instant, he said quite simply,—

"If we never meet again, Miss Ballinger, pray remember that you brought happiness into at least one obscure New England home. We shall think of your visit here with gratitude, and often talk of it, my mother and I. Good-bye."

Firm, self-contained to the end, his voice betrayed no emotion, as he raised her hand respectfully to his lips. She said nothing. What could she say? Then he turned; the white face, the shrunk, shadowy figure vanished in the gloaming; and that was the last she saw of Saul Barham.

In a ground-floor "parlour" at "The Brunswick" late the following afternoon—a parlour, heavily decorated, and brilliant with electric light, Grace fell into Mrs. Frampton's expansive embrace. It was a bitterly cold day, and the cheek which her niece pressed seemed frozen. It belonged to a short stout woman, still almost as vigorous as at twenty, with iron-grey hair, that rose in crip waves, and broke over the broad prominent forehead, indicating stubborn natural force. Swift black eyes, a healthy colour, fine white teeth, told the same tale of strong vitality. The expanded nostril, and full mobile mouth, showed, perhaps other, but not contradictory, characteristics.

Impossible to doubt that this was a clever, dominant, possibly at times a violent woman; attractive to some, to others a terror, and a *bête noire*. Voluble, beyond the limits of discretion, yet rarely foolish; impulsive as a child, loving and hating with equal intensity, yet prudent, worldly-wise, humorous, and quick-sighted; it was not difficult to form an idea, more or less just, of Mrs. Frampton, in five minutes' conversation. But then as her nephew said, "Aunt Susan always lets herself go." It was that quality of "letting herself go" which made her so entertaining a companion.

She spoke rapidly, in a high but not unmusical voice, holding her niece out at arm's length after embracing her, while she scanned the girl's countenance.

"You look well, my child! This horrible climate agrees with you, then? I have been shrivelling up visibly every hour since I landed. And then the awful heat of these furnaces! I thought I should be roasted alive in the railway carriage coming here! How can you stand it?"

"I grin and bear it as well as I can, Aunt Su. And as to the climate, I like this dry cold a great deal better than the damp and fog of London."

She shrugged her shoulders. "'Quel drôle de goût!' as the irreverent Frenchman said when someone spoke of the Jews as 'God's chosen people!' Mordy has been talking the same nonsense. As if the London climate was not good enough for any living creature, except perhaps, an asthmatic poodle! My nerves are all rasped here. I hate it."

"Well, Aunty, we won't rasp you more, by saying anything about the climate, but we mean to make you like the country very much."

"Never!" she cried, in a melodramatic tone. "Except the Hurlstones' house, everything I have seen is hideous. Those dreadful streets! You didn't say half enough about those dreadful New York streets. I felt as if every bone in my body was dislocated, when I drove through them! And then their way of spitting about one. There was one man who actually aimed across me at a spittoon! Pray, have you got accustomed to *that?*"

"I never see it," returned Grace, with a smile. "You know I am one of those stupid but happy people who don't see ugly things unless they are thrust under their very nose."

"Well, my dear, this *was* thrust under my very nose. No, I hate all I have seen of the people, except the Hurlstones. I except *them*, for they are thoroughly well-bred, nice people, and their house is charming."

"There are plenty of houses as good— indeed, better, to my taste—and plenty of people as nice."

"You didn't do them justice, Gracey, in your letters to me. They are a charming family. I was most agreeably surprised in Beatrice Hurlstone. She would hold her own in any London drawing-room."

"I didn't say she would not, Aunty. I am sure I said nothing against them. I was very grateful for all their kindness and hospitality."

"Oh! grateful. We know what *that* means. You didn't like them, and you put Mordy off from liking the girl."

"My dear aunt! What nonsense! As if anything I could say would influence him in the slightest degree in that way! He flirted with her at first, and then he found someone he admired more."

"That is just it. If he *will* marry an American, I'd rather it was Beatrice Hurlstone than anyone. I don't at all like the idea of Miss Planter whom he raves to me about. He shan't marry her, if I can help it. In the first place, I am told she is a desperate flirt. Then her father is one of those speculators, who is rich to-day, and may be poor to-morrow, and will only give his daughter an income—will settle nothing upon her. Whereas Mr. Hurlstone's large fortune will be divided equally between his son and his daughter—he told me so himself."

"That was considerate of him," said Grace, with one of her rare touches of sarcasm.

And the hero of their talk entering the room at that moment, there was an abrupt change in the conversation.

"I find her looking very well, Mordy!" cried his aunt. "Is it the New England parsonage that has given her those roses? She looked like a squeezed lemon four months ago."

"Oh! twenty-four hours at sea picked her up. She is an awfully good sailor, and never missed a meal; and amused herself, I can tell you, 'pretty considerable,' as we say over here—having three men, all very much gone on her."

Mrs. Frampton laughed heartily.

"And you have been staying with the parents of one of them—the young man you say is a prig?"

"I didn't say that," responded Grace quickly, "I said *you* might call him so. He is a very remarkable young man, and I like him exceedingly; but I am much afraid he will not live long. He is sadly changed, even since we were on board ship together. His poor mother's face haunts me. He is her only son."

The mocking expression of Aunt Susan's countenance changed while her niece was speaking. The eyes were veiled with a tender sympathy, which contrasted curiously with their habitual outlook. She, too, had known what this sorrow meant, long years ago.

"Poor woman! And is there nothing to be done?"

"Perhaps if he went to a warm climate, and gave up his professorship, he might recover, but that is just what he won't do."

"Then he doesn't really love his mother!" she cried, impatiently. "These Americans are all alike—can't rest—must fret themselves to fiddle-strings. The idea of a man sacrificing his life to his work! It is positively wicked."

"I suspect he is a romantic sort of cove who fancies there is only one woman in the world," said her nephew, fixing his eyes on Grace. "If he is disappointed, he doesn't care to live.

I have known one chap like that. It's very rum."

His sister said nothing. She rose and went to the window, where the curtains had not been dropped before the gas-lit street. A well-appointed brougham stood at the door. Grace thought she recognized the horses; and at the same moment the negro waiter entered and asked if the ladies were at home to Mrs. Courtly.

"Certainly," said Mrs. Frampton. Then, as the man disappeared, "I hear she is a delightful person—not only from Mordy, but others."

"I am glad you hear that,' said Grace, smiling. "She *is* a delightful person, but many women are jealous of her, and you might have heard, as I did, that she is only delightful to men, which is not the least true."

The object of these remarks entered, swathed in velvet and silver-fox, and redolent of Parma violets. Her bright smile, graceful manner, and musical voice could not but dispose favourably one as sensitive to impressions as Mrs. Frampton.

"I do not feel that we are strangers—

you have been so good to my children," she said.

Mrs. Courtly responded in a like strain, and then,—

"I suppose I ought to apologize for calling on you just as you have arrived from a long journey, Mrs. Frampton, but I wanted to engage you all to dine with me to-morrow. I know you are to be here but a few days, and you must see something of our society—we think ourselves very nice, you know. I say 'we' though I don't belong to Boston—only come in occasionally from my solitude, for a little social relaxation."

"Solitude! I like that!" laughed Ballinger. "I don't believe you are ever alone, Mrs. Courtly. I am sure you have a regular succession of representative men and women: literature, fashion, and the fine arts, they all go to you, and you take them in."

"That is a doubtful compliment," and the American lady gave a rippling laugh; "but I am afraid it is the truth. I do take them in—that is, the representatives of literature and the fine arts. They think I know something—I am just clever enough never to *do* anything—

and so they do not discover what a fraud I am. As to fashion, oh, I can be frivolous enough, as you have seen. There is no sham about *that*."

"I am glad to hear it," said Mrs. Frampton, nodding her head, "for I am frivolous, too—frivolous and worldly, as this very superior young woman, my niece, is always pointing out to me."

"What a detestable creature you make me out! Happily Mrs. Courtly knows me a little. When did you come to Boston, Mrs. Courtly, and where are you staying?"

"I am at the Vendôme, where I always go. I came on Saturday, and have been hunting up some of my friends, to meet you to-morrow. On Wednesday, if agreeable to you, we will dine at the Country Club, where they have a little informal dance ending at eleven o'clock, once a week. I think it will amuse you. If it snows, which it threatens to do to-night, we will go in sleighs."

Mrs. Frampton looked petrified.

"What! in evening dress?"

"Why, yes! We wrap up well, with fur hoods and double veils—and wear frocks that won't tumble ; and the drive back, under a full moon, as we have now, will be delightful."

"Well," said Mrs. Frampton, dubiously, " I never did anything so skittish when I was young —and now that I am an old woman—what if I am upset ? "

" Oh ! you won't be upset—and if you were, it wouldn't hurt you. You have no distance to fall, and in the soft white snow—"

" Good heavens ! The very idea of it sends cold water down my back. No, thank you. *They* shall go, but you must excuse *me*. A nocturnal sleighing party—returning from a ball —running races, I dare say—no, thank you— not for me ! "

Mrs. Courtly's predictions were verified. The snow came down heavily before morning. The streets were blocked ; the tramcars moved stealthily along. Then it froze, and every one who ventured from his door wore snow-shoes, spiked in the soles, to obtain some hold on the white surface, slippery as glass, and glistening in the noon-day sun.

CHAPTER V.

That morning, at breakfast in the public room, Mrs. Frampton was outraged at having a glass of iced water and an orange given to her, before the tea was served.

"What does the man give me an orange for, such a morning as this ? As to this iced water, I would not touch a drop of it, in any weather —I hope you have, neither of you, taken to that dangerous habit ?"

Then, as the negro in attendance leant reflectively on the back of Grace's chair, his round eyes fixed upon the animated face of the speaker. "May I ask," she continued, "if that gentleman of colour always listens to your conversation ? Perhaps he would join in, if you asked him."

"It's a way they have here," murmured her nephew. "They don't mean to be cheeky, but servants here are the only class who *never* by any accident address you as 'sir.' As to these waiter-fellows, their manners, I admit, are peculiar. One darky pulled my hat off my head the other day. He thought he was doing the civil thing."

She threw up her hands. "And pray, did you do the civil thing in return?" The *menu* for the morning meal being handed to her, she exclaimed, "Good heavens! What is this? 'Clam Chouder,' 'Squab Pie.' What on earth is 'Squab Pie?' 'Cold Slaw and Shredden Beef!'—It sounds like cannibalism!—'Flap Jacks, and Maple Syrup! a combination of fish and trees, I suppose! 'Waffles!' 'Buckwheat Cakes!' 'Grits!' 'Dip Toast!'— Is that another word for 'pap'?"—and so on, with a running commentary, down the bill of fare.

Some of these unknown dishes, however, she tried, and candidly owned were excellent, and when the breakfast was dispatched, and they had returned to their own "parlour," Mrs. Frampton was visibly better disposed towards the outer world. She moved one of the ponderous chairs to the window, and produced a long roll of embroidery.

"That is what I have not seen a woman do, since I arrived in the States," said Mordaunt.

"I dare say they work a great deal in strict private, but never in public. They don't consider it 'the thing,' I believe. They are very angry when I say so, but it is the truth."

"Well, there is no great virtue that I can see, in doing this sort of rubbish," said his aunt, in her most amiable manner. "If I could do anything more useful, I should. But I can talk much better when I am pulling something about; and Grace and I are going to have a long gossip, while you go and smoke your cigar, and bring us back the news, out of one of those dreadful, wicked papers."

"You're a regular Eve, Aunt Su," laughed her nephew, as he sauntered to the door. "The woman tempted me, and I did eat."

"Ah! Adam was a poor creature," returned Mrs. Frampton, as she put on her spectacles; then, when he had left the room. "I am not at all satisfied about Mordy," she continued, as she stabbed the canvas with her needle, and a stream of sanguinary *filoselle* followed it.

"Why, Aunty?"

"Don't you see how much more silent he is, with only an occasional burst of his old fun? I am afraid he cares—*really* cares—for this girl."

"And if he does, what then? There is really nothing to object to in her. Putting her beauty aside, she is clever—in her way—wonderfully adaptable, and has a great deal of character. I don't say that she is exactly the sister-in-law I should have selected, but then, almost certainly, the girl I should prefer, Mordy would not look at. If Miss Planter makes up her mind to marry him, which I am not at all sure that she will—"

"The idea! Not accept Mordy, who might marry almost anyone in England?"

"Nonsense, Aunty. You know very well that, judged by your own standard—the worldly standard—a poor baronet, without any transcendent abilities to advance his career, is not a match for ambitious mammas or daughters to jump at. If dear Mordy really and truly falls in love at last with this American girl, and that she returns his love—she won't marry him unless she does—I see no reason why they should not be very happy."

"I wish it had been the Hurlstone girl," said Mrs. Frampton, without taking her eyes from her work. "Besides the money being certain in her case, there are the relations. The

Planters, I am told, are people of yesterday."

"Yesterday, or the day before, does it make much difference?"

"The father, I am told, is impossible. The mother—"

"You heard all this from the Hurlstones; it is a tainted source. People are even more jealous of each other over here, it seems to me, than in London. And in this case, you see, there are peculiar reasons for jealousy. If you meet the Planters in the course of our travels" (she cautiously avoided any hint of the Californian rendezvous), "you must not be prejudiced. You must judge the girl upon her own merits. Promise me you will do this, Aunty."

"Oh! No one can say I am prejudiced. That is the last charge that can be brought against me." Grace bit her lip, and bent her head over a dropped stitch in her knitting. There was a little pause; Mrs. Frampton heaved a sigh, then stretching out her hand to her work-basket, drew from the depths of it a society paper, not yet a fortnight old. "Look here, Gracey," she continued, as she opened and flattened out the paper with her hand, "there is a subject upon which I have long since given up speaking to you. I shouldn't do so now, but for something Mordy said to me yesterday. I had hoped your eyes were gradually opened to Mr. Ivor Lawrence's true character. I told Mordy to tell you the common topic of conversation; the new light that has been thrown upon the case. And now, as it seems you still believe in the man, I think you should see this paragraph," and she handed the paper to her niece. It ran thus:—

"With regard to the disputed will of the late Mr. Tracy, which promises to be a *cause célèbre*, we understand that the attorney who drew up several wills for the deceased between the years 1875 and 1887, has been traced to Victoria, where he emigrated on account of his health. He is subpœnaed to appear, and will form an important witness, as it is said he brings with him duplicates of these wills, which appear to have been destroyed. The evidence of this witness, as testifying to the affection which subsisted formerly between Mr. Giles Tracy and his uncle, will, it is said, be of paramount importance on the trial."

Mrs. Frampton's eye was fixed upon her niece

as Grace read this; but she did not wince. She folded the paper carefully, and returned it to her aunt.

"Thank you; it makes no difference—I am sure you did not expect that it would—in my opinion. It would be the same if Mr. Lawrence lost his case. I *know* he is incapable of having used his influence with his uncle to induce him to alter his will."

"Humph! There are grave doubts whether it is not *forged*." Grace gave a little contemptuous smile. "I am told he has been given the cold shoulder at his club—one man cut him dead—and he goes nowhere."

"No; if he did, he would have come to us."

Mrs. Frampton pulled her needle so irritably through the canvas, that the silk nearly snapped.

"Thank goodness he has not. If he had behaved like a gentleman, and come forward immediately his uncle died, it might be difficult to shake him off now. As it is, he cut the Gordian knot himself."

"We will not go over the old ground again, Aunt. The trial is public property; I can't help hearing it discussed. But that question of his 'coming forward,' please, must never be spoken of. Just think how inconsistent you are, dear. You suggest that he forged; and then say he would have behaved like a gentleman, if, having forged, he had 'come forward.' The fact is, Ivor Lawrence is a very proud, sensitive man. I believe the tenour of his uncle's will was a surprise to him, and, when he was told it was to be disputed, and the charge that was to be made against him, he resolved to subject none of his friends to the ordeal of receiving a suspected man, until the trial was over. And now, dear aunt, please let the subject be closed as far as I am personally concerned. You are the only person who knows something of what I have suffered. But I have been lighter-hearted and braver since I left England. And why? Simply because time, instead of shaking my belief in the man whom all the world suspects, has made it stronger. At first his silence crushed me. If I thought my friend unworthy, I should still be crushed, far more than at first. But, you see, I am crushed no longer. Be content with that."

She had risen, and was standing before her aunt, who looked up, over her spectacles, literally dumfounded; until she felt two strong young arms flung round her neck, and a shower of kisses upon her cheek. That was an argument she never could resist. She patted the girl's back with one fat dimpled hand, while she wiped away a furtive tear with the other.

"God bless you, child! You are too good and noble—yes, too noble for this wretched, miserable world of ours."

And so peace was restored between the two women, who, being very unlike, were yet warmly attached to each other.

Later, they went forth with Mordaunt, and walked across the park, on planks laid upon the pathway, up to Beacon Street, and were reminded of Bath, as one looks down from its century-old crescent; and then they crunched the frozen snow under their spiked shoes, back to the Museum of Fine Arts, where they found a collection of Blake's strange and poetic conceptions, and some memorable sketches, by W. M. Hunt, an American of rare genius, lately deceased, and but little known in this country. Copley's portraits—our Lord Lyndhurst's father—of which there are so few examples in England, also interested them;

and, of course, there were the usual inevitable French pictures, which are the staple commodity of all collections in the States. They passed a pleasant hour here; after which, Mrs. Frampton was deposited at the Brunswick, as she declared nothing would induce her to enter the electric car which was to convey her nephew and niece into the heart of the city.

"I have looked inside one," she said, "that is enough! I saw a double row of people standing up in the middle, clinging on by straps, and jammed against the knees of those who were seated! Never saw anything so shocking in my life. No, thank you. I will go in a carriage, or on my ten toes, or I will remain at home. None of those dreadful tramways for me!"

So they left her, and went their ways. And in the course of their ways they ran up against Mordaunt's wiry friend, Reid. He said he had come to Boston for a few days' visit to his mother, "who will be very happy to call on you, Miss Ballinger, if you will allow her." And when Grace had expressed her willingness to be called upon, he continued, "She is a real good woman, my mother; but you must be prepared for some tall talk. It don't amount to much, but it takes a little time to get accustomed to it."

That evening the party assembled by Mrs. Courtly to meet her English friends was peculiarly agreeable. Besides Mr. Laffan and other distinguished men, were three ladies; one, a poetess whose stirring verse had moved a whole nation's heart, and two sisters whose well-earned reputation for brilliancy had won for them the name of "The Duplex Burners."

Mrs. Frampton was at her best. She was always appreciative of talent, more especially of conversational talent, and would toss into the cauldron, now and again, a pungent remark which stimulated alike the powers of the artists and the appetites of those who sat at meat.

The talk turning upon American modes of spelling, she said, in her trenchant way,—

"I should have been whipped, when I was a child, if I had spelt theatre, *t-e-r* instead of *tre*. Why, it is neither Latin nor any other tongue!"

"We let 'the dead past bury its dead'!" was the reply. "We follow the living tongues, the tongues in your head and mine, and those distinctly say 'thea-*ter*.' We don't approve of whipping little girls for spelling as they pronounce, even if the result be to produce such brilliant women as yourself," with a bow.

Mrs. Frampton was reduced to silence for a moment by this un-English compliment, and so her ear caught another that was being proffered to Grace. Her niece was deploring the loss of the letter *u* in so many words as now printed in America.

"Do you really like the *u* dropped in such a word as 'parlour'?" she asked of her neighbour.

"I prefer a parlour with *you* in it," he replied.

Grace laughed.

"You are trying to silence me, I see. But do tell me why you *will* change our c's into s's, in such words as 'offence' and 'defence'?"

"I suppose we think that in 'offence' and 'defence' you English are always *at sea!*" returned her incorrigible neighbour.

And so the chaff went on.

One man present sustained theories which, as coming from an American, were curious. He declared there was over-education in his country, and used all the arguments in support of this view which would have been employed by an old English Tory.

Mordaunt Ballinger stared when he heard a citizen of the United States declare that muscle and sinew were not yet driven out of the field by machinery, that scientific absorption was an evil, and that the world's work cannot be done by the brain alone. It was a little too much, even for the young Conservative member, when this clever supporter of paradoxes maintained that people would be happier if they knew less, and that genius was more sure to rise from a poor educational plane than from a highly cultivated one.

"Certainly," assented another, "our most successful men in the country have *not* been the best educated."

"Theirs was a rich soil," continued the first speaker, " that needed no top-dressing. It was just suited to the grain it had to grow. Its strength was concentrated on that. Manured with learning, all manner of rank, useless stuff would have sprung up, and flourished there."

"For shame!" said Mrs. Courtly's silvery voice. "I wonder you dare to talk such blasphemy, almost within the shadow of Harvard! To think that I should live to hear a Bostonian throw such an aspersion on 'Belles Letters.'"

"Ah! dear lady, but 'Belles Letters,' like other feminine things, are so apt to distract our minds from the only serious object of life, which, of course, is money-getting!"

This elicited hisses and laughter, in which the speaker himself joined. *Il N'y a que la verité qui blesse.* Boston could never take such an accusation to itself.

"One would fancy you were from Chicago!" said Mrs. Courtly.

Now Chicago is to the Bostonians as the full moon is to a dog; they are never tired of baying at it.

"Well, then, I *am* from Chicago. I was there two weeks ago on business. And what do you suppose I saw in a shop-window? I can tell you it was something worth going to Chicago to see. Why, a statue of the Venus de Medici in a Jäger's combination suit!"

"Great Scott!" cried a man from the further end of the table, "Jäger must be like the poet, *nascitur* but *non fit*. Poor Goddess! 'To what base uses we may return, Horatio!' But we are a practical people. Beauty and utility with us go hand in hand. Indeed, you see that in this case they don't stop *there*."

" No," said one of the ladies gravely. " Life has never been the same to me since I saw Lord Byron's head, with a chestnut wig upon it, in a 'tonsorial saloon,' and a bust of the young Augustus at an optician's, with a pair of blue spectacles on his nose ! "

Mrs. Frampton, meantime, was being questioned by her neighbour as to the route the travellers meant to take in going westward.

" I suppose you go through Chicago ? " he said.

" Ask my nephew. I am as dough in his hands, and the dough is unleavened. It doesn't *rise* in the oven of your railway carriages. I dread the journey. By-the-bye, why *will* you call them 'cars'? My idea of a 'car' is the thing I remember as a child in my Roman history, Tullia trampling her father to death. You know—and so on."

" We don't trample our fathers, even when they are very much in the way ; but we like short cuts, for all that. Now 'car' is a short cut for a long carriage-drive."

"Oh! but I beg to say you don't *always* go in for shortness. You call a 'lift' an 'elevator,' and you always 'conclude' a thing, instead of 'ending' it. I must tell you frankly that we think those long words horrid."

"I am sorry for it," he replied, amused; "but we, on our side, think fashionable English slang, and a good deal of fashionable English pronunciation, horrid. There is a lady here, lately returned from London, who speaks so beautifully that we can't understand more than half she says!"

Mrs. Frampton laughed. She was quite pleased with her neighbour. If he carried the war into the enemy's country, she felt justified in saying a tart thing.

"You mean that she no longer pronounces 'clerk' as if it rhymed with 'shirk' and 'work.' You get that and the tendency to nasal intonation from your Puritan fathers. We retain a Roundhead broadness and boldness of utterance."

"Ah! I see the broadness and boldness," returned the American, with a humorous twitch of the lips. "Still, all evidence shows that Englishmen of Chaucer's day pronounced 'clerk' as it is written."

"Chaucer? Good Heavens! You don't expect us to go on talking as they did in Edward the Third's reign?"

"Why are you to start from Charles II. rather than Edward III? '*Clark*' is an affectation that crept into the language in the last century, when it became the fashion to talk of *Jarsey*, and *Barkley*. The latter I believe you still retain in fashionable parlance."

"Of course! The man or woman would be lost who spoke of *Berkley* Square."

"But worse than all is your fashionable pronunciation of Pall Mall. Why! you lose all the pleasant old association and courtly flavour of the 'Palace Mall,' by calling it 'Pell Mell.' You might as well call it 'Helter-Skelter!'"

"Don't talk to me of association, or accuracy, or grammar, or anything else. Custom overrides all with us."

"The trouble is that you will not allow it to do so with us," he returned, smiling.

"Really, I think we might be allowed to know how to speak our own language!"

"Not if you go on changing it all the time, according to the vagaries of fashion. When *we* have gotten hold of a word, we stick to it. Look at that poor word 'genteel,' which was such a useful servant to you all through the last century, and now you have kicked it into the gutter!"

"It deserved kicking into the gutter. It had become so frayed and tarnished that it wasn't fit to wear. We have incorporated a number of new words into the language, so no one can complain because we discard one or two."

"If the new ones supplied the vacuum, but they do not. You have no word to replace 'genteel.' Your argument reminds me of a man who having lost his boots, put on two hats and an overcoat!"

Thus they sparred amicably through that pleasant dinner, the least animated member of which beyond a doubt was Mordaunt Ballinger. And yet he sat beside Mrs. Courtly, whom he sincerely liked, and who, though she tried to make the conversation general, found an opportunity to say to him,—

"I have heard of our friends' arrival at Pittsburg."

"Do they speak of going to California?" he asked quickly.

"Mrs. Planter's cough was worse as soon as she got home," replied Mrs. Courtly with a smile. "That promises well."

CHAPTER VI.

Mrs. Reid called the next day with her son. She was a solid-looking lady of rather severe aspect, with spectacles, as unlike as possible to her thin, quick-witted son. Mordaunt was out, and Mrs. Frampton, knowing that the American was the friend who had given him a good deal of advice as to investments, tackled him at once, leaving his mother to be entertained by Grace. Mrs. Frampton riddled him through with her questions; but he was equal to the occasion, and came so triumphantly out of the ordeal, that she accepted with alacrity Mrs. Reid's verbal invitation to dine with her the following day.

"You will not expect a large party,"—Mrs. Reid trod heavily on each word, as she spoke—" My friend Lady Clydesdale and one or two others will be with me. But as I understand your nephew purposes leaving Boston in quite a few days, I was anxious to secure the pleasure of receiving you, if possible."

At Lady Clydesdale's name, Grace had frowned and shaken her head at her aunt, but it was no use. Miss Ballinger even went so far as to say,—

"I am afraid that *I*—"

But Mrs. Frampton nipped her in the bud.

"Nonsense! my dear. We have no engagement, and I can't possibly leave you at home. My nephew would be extremely sorry to miss your hospitable invitation, Mrs. Reid. We shall be delighted to dine with you."

And when they were gone, she said,—

"I like that man. He is very shrewd. He may be valuable to Mordy. I wouldn't miss dining with them for the world. As to your wanting to refuse because Lady Clydesdale is to be there, it is too foolish! The woman can't eat you."

"I should disagree with her if she did," laughed Grace. "Of course, if you and Mordy both want to go, I am ready to sacrifice myself, as I did, indeed, just now. You left me to Mrs. Reid's mercy, and she has very little. Her son prepared me for her 'tall talk;' but its height did not impress me so much as its weight. Between her and Lady Clydesdale, you will carry home nothing of me but a few mangled remains."

That same day two of their agreeable acquaintances of the previous evening escorted them to the State House, with its gilded dome, and fine eighteenth-century decorations. They ascended a lofty tower, and gained a comprehensive view of the city, the winding river, and Charlestown, and beyond it the south coast, and island-sprinkled sea. It was a clear, brilliant day, though intensely cold. The dark boats on the glittering river, the numerous vanes and pinnacles that rose above the snow-bound city, and caught the sunlight, the forest of masts in the harbour, and silhouettes of wide-armed elms upon the common, the frozen lake on which hundreds were skating and sliding merrily, and over all a span of wind-swept sky, almost Florentine in its hard, blue depth, startled the English travellers with unexpected beauty.

"This is really charming!" cried Mrs. Frampton. And after such an admission there was nothing more to be said.

Then they visited several "book stores," and the noble public library. At last, when the sky was growing the colour of a tea-rose, against which church tower and steeple uprose in solid purple, they recrossed the park, and Grace and Mordaunt hastened to dress for the Country Club dinner.

At six o'clock a double sleigh drove to the door, with a great jingling of bells, and servants fur-capped and coated; and inside the open shell-shaped carriage two figures, one a bundle of Shetland veils and sable, out of which Mrs. Courtly's silvery voice arose, the other an attenuated stroke of black, like a note of admiration, as he leapt out and stood upright in the snow. This proved to be John Reid.

The brother and sister were equally pleased to find their brisk American friend of the party, and Mrs. Courtly explained that he had called on her late in the afternoon, when she had been so fortunate as to find he could fill the seat left suddenly vacant. She added in a whisper to Grace, while the two men were talking,—

"His mother always tries to prevent his calling on me, if he is in Boston when I happen to be here. She will be extremely angry at our carrying him off to-night."

The moon had not yet risen, and the drive to the Country Club in the dark would have seemed long, but for the ball of talk tossed to and fro. Mrs. Courtly was in her brightest and youngest mood, ready to enjoy, and therefore to make others enjoy, everything. They drove at length through some gates into a small park, and, at the tail of several other sleighs, alighted at a long house, surrounded by a wide balcony or "piazza," into which all the rooms on the ground floor opened. None were very large, and in nearly all small round tables were laid for dinner, so as to accommodate parties of four and six separately. Some were already occupied, some were awaiting the descent of the ladies from their tiring-chamber.

Nearly everyone had arrived, and the whole place was alive with light and bustle, greetings in merry, high-pitched voices; waiters, heavily laden, charging to and fro through the crowd; men with frozen moustaches thawing before the bright wood fires; nymphs in procession down the stairs, emerging miraculously fresh from their hoods and mantles.

The dinner was excellent, and the spirit in which it was evident that every one sat down to it was that proper to all entertainment, but which so often with us is conspicuous by its absence. They came, young and old, with the resolute intention of amusing themselves. If they had not "felt like" amusing themselves, they would have stayed away. Look round the room, and you could see nowhere that air of resignation, that air which says, "Though I should drop with fatigue and *ennui*, I will go through with it, never fear!"—which is so piteous on the faces, nay, on the very backs o so many British chaperons. It is true there were but few of these. Two and three girls could come with one matron, leaving their respective mothers at home. If the mothers came, it was because they liked it; in some instances, because they meant to dance themselves. This gaiety of temperament and power of enjoyment was, of course, yet more remarkable when, after dinner—and a little interval for digestion, coffee, and cigars—men and women re-assembled in a pretty ball-room upstairs. The hilarity then seemed infectious. Mordaunt had not appeared so animated since he had parted from Clare Planter. He danced with all the prettiest girls; was pronounced to be "too nice for anything," and encountered, in consequence, some scowls from jealous swains. At first it was only the young who "took the floor." But soon elderly gentlemen and mature dowagers were to be seen advancing, and receding, and gyrating, in the complicated movements of the waltz and polka, as naturalized in America. Mrs. Courtly, after presenting half a dozen men to Grace, was carried off by a youth, renowned for his dancing, and who always declared that no one waltzed like her. This was followed by "Dancing in the Barn," which Mordaunt had been taught at Brackley, and which he and Mrs. Courtly now performed greatly to their own satisfaction and that of the few spectators who were not themselves prancing round the room. Among those few were Grace and John Reid.

"Wouldn't my mother be down on Mrs. Courtly, if she could see her?" he said, laughing.

"What for? For making herself and others happy?"

"Why, yes, in *a way*," he replied, still

chuckling. "You see, she is kinder severe, as we Yankees say, on Mrs. Courtly, who, *she* declares, tries to captivate every man she comes near. I tell her it wants no trying, we all take to Mrs. Courtly as ducks do to water. That makes my mother mad."

"I hope Boston is not very censorious?"

"Well, you see, I don't live in Boston," he replied, with becoming caution. "There are quite a number of sets here, and, as in other big cities, I suppose, they sit on each other—rather. My mother belongs to the earnest set. 'There are no flies on *her*.' (Have you heard the Salvation Army hymn? Well, I won't repeat it. It would shock you.) She is a real good woman, and spends all her time rummaging about at committees, and schools, and hospitals. The trouble is, she expects every one to have the same tastes, and can't tolerate what she calls 'frivolity.'"

"Then she will not tolerate *me*. I do nothing useful. Do you come often to Boston?"

"Once or twice a year, for a few days. In the summer my mother meets me at Newport, or we cross the ocean together. I allow I like that better than coming here, where my mother's friends are—well—not quite my style."

Then a man came up and claimed Grace's hand for "the German," and she had no further opportunity of hearing Mr. Reid's views. The dance was over at eleven o'clock; and now began once more a rapid eclipse of all the meteors, in their shining array, under soft but solid clouds of fur; and outside there was a jingling of bells, a champing of bits, and stamping of hoofs on the frozen snow, and the white moonlight streamed down over all, glistening like silver on the icicles that depended from the balcony, and articulating every object in blue-black shadow on the snow.

The drive back was like a fairy dream, with this advantage, it was exhilarating, while dreams often enervate, leaving their recipient, on waking, less well able to cope with hard, prosaic fact. They flew along in procession, with their clanging bells, over the burnished snow, every leafless twig told out in tracery of shadow on the roadway, every "sentinel pine," equipped in white fur, standing erect and motionless against the still, blue night. The moon was at its full, and smote the foreheads of the little painted, wooden houses with its blinding light, and flooded the distant country, lifting blue hills, on the horizon, into that prominence which vagueness lends to outlines, from which the eye in sunlight is distracted by a thousand small intervening details.

"It was perfect enchantment!" said Grace to her aunt the next morning at breakfast.

"Yes, it was awfully jolly," said her brother. "And then Reid is such a good sort. We were lucky to have him with us. Some of these young chaps, I find, are very jealous of one. Such rot, you know. I overheard one of them say to a girl whom I had asked to dance, 'Of course *we* have none of us any chance *now*. You'll want to dance with the Englishman all the time!' I should like to have kicked him."

"Never mind about *them*; they don't interest me," said Mrs. Frampton. "Tell me what Mr. Reid said. Did you ask him anything about 'Readings' or 'Central Pacifics'?"

"Bless you! no, Aunt Su. Fancy talking of investments *en parti carré* with Mrs. Courtly. She would have stopped the sleigh and have begged us to get out."

Mrs. Reid's dinner that evening in her magnificent house in Commonwealth Avenue was as typical, in its way, as Mrs Courtly's had been. There were six guests, besides Lady Clydesdale, invited to meet our English friends, and most of them appeared to be persons devoted, body and soul, to some one scientific, religious, or philanthropic cause. Genuine enthusiasm about anything is too rare for me to indulge in a little cheap satire about it. Four of these guests struck both Mrs. Frampton and Grace as kindly, honest-minded men and women, not stuck up with the vanity of well-doing, but with intelligence perhaps a little unduly inflamed over the propagation or extermination of something or other. The fifth was Miss Lobb, who was as drastic, as universal, and as unrelenting in her questions, as she had been on board the *Teutonic*. The sixth was a merry little spinster of forty, with a cropped head, and eye-brows like circumflex accents, who seemed strangely out of place in that serious assembly, until it transpired that she wrote for the daily papers —was what is there called an "Editor," which only means the caterer of certain branches of information. Being a protégée of Mrs. Reid's, she was invited to her table whenever there was "copy" to be picked up. Her name was Pie, which gave rise to a number of facile jokes among her friends—and she had many : for she was always good-humoured, never wounded anyone by her writing, and was often extremely serviceable to Mrs. Reid and others in airing the views and projects they desired to make public. Mordaunt, who took Mrs. Reid in to dinner, had Miss Pie on his other side. Mrs. Reid naturally sat at the head of her table ; but the party being of twelve, it was impossible, in the alternation of guests, that her son should sit opposite her. He took Lady Clydesdale in to dinner, and placed her on his left, facing Mrs. Reid ; Grace on his right, found, to her extreme annoyance, that she was not only next but one to Lady Clydesdale, but from her position close to the angle, could not avoid conversation with her country-woman, if it was thrust upon her.

Next to Grace was an ancient bachelor of great wealth and boundless liberality, who had founded and endowed several charitable institutions, and whose purse-strings were so readily untied that he was attacked by every promoter of beneficence in turn. He took Mrs. Frampton in to dinner; upon whose left sat an eminent doctor. Then came Mrs. Reid, dominating the table; and on the other side, next to Miss Pie, an Unitarian minister, naturally voluble, but utterly quelled by Miss Lobb, who was next him. The individual who sat between this terrible lady—before whom most men fled—and Lady Clydesdale was a business man, to whom she devoted most of her attention during dinner.

It had not advanced far when the hostess, placing her heavy artillery into position, directed a slow shot at Mrs. Frampton.

"I regret that, during your too brief stay here, you should not have come into contact with the higher educational and progressive life of Boston, Mrs. Frampton. I have been deploring to Sir Mordaunt Ballinger that he should have seen only the frivolous side of our society. There is another; that of culture, that of philosophical investigation, that of enthusiasm for humanity. These are not to be found at country-club balls."

"No. They would be rather out of place

there. But you have given us enough of all those good things here to-night, to readjust the balance, I fancy."

And Mrs. Frampton said this with a pleasant smile, which—probably to all but Miss Pie—robbed the rejoinder of any latent satire.

The benevolent old bachelor on her left here claimed her attention with a remark, which left Mrs. Reid no choice but to withdraw her field-pieces. She turned to her right.

Mordaunt had been talking for the last few minutes to the bright little spinster. He found a hand laid heavily upon his arm, and a voice hurtled past him,—

"My dear Pie, I cannot allow you to monopolize Sir Mordaunt *entirely*—she is a savoury Pie, but must be cut sometimes—you forgive my little joke, dear? I was going to tell you, Sir Mordaunt, of my disappointment in not having secured the most delightful woman to meet you this evening; the person of all others who is a representative of what is noblest, most cultivated, most advanced among American women."

"Ah!" exclaimed Mordaunt, maliciously.

"Of course I know whom you mean. That description can only refer to *one* woman."

"Do you mean that you have *met* her?" this with heavy-eyed surprise.

"Of course I have. Mrs. Courtly and I are great friends."

She threw up her hands; and at the same moment caught Lady Clydesdale's eye, by inclining her head a little to one side.

"That woman!" she almost groaned. Then she leant forward, and said down the table with solemnity,—

"My dear Lady Clydesdale, will you tell your countryman here, that we have nobler types of womanhood than Mrs. Courtly; that in our earnest seeking after the light we entirely repudiate that class of person—worldly pleasure-seekers, whose influence over the youth of both sexes we hold to be very pernicious."

John Reid and Mordaunt exchanged glances, and in John's was the faintest indication of a twinkle.

"I should not esteem this country as I do, if it were made up of Mrs. Courtlys!" said Lady Clydesdale, severely.

"Widows, who only think of ensnaring men!" cried Miss Lobb.

"Come, my dear," said the merry little Pie, "you and I do just the same, all the time, only we don't succeed as well."

There was some natural laughter at this, but Mrs. Reid could not encourage levity on so grave a subject.

"At her time of life," she said, "still to court the society of the young and giddy—to dance and flirt as she does! Mrs. Frampton, I trust you understand that is not the stamp of woman *we* approve of."

"Really? Well, it is very difficult to please every one. She seems to please a great many."

"*Too* many! That is the trouble," this with an ominous shake of the head. "Men are so easily deluded!"

"She does not only charm men," said Grace, who felt it was cowardly to remain longer silent; "she can delight women also. She is the most many-sided person I have ever met—with a great deal more depth than people give her credit for."

"My! what bravery!" chuckled Miss Pie, under her breath.

"No one doubts her *depth*," rejoined Lady Clydesdale, sarcastically, "but everyone knows you have peculiar opinions, Miss Ballinger, about—conduct, both in men and women. If you like people, you defend them, no matter what they do."

"How ought I to behave when I hear *you* abused, Lady Clydesdale?" she asked, white with anger, for she had a premonition of what was coming.

"Time enough for that when I have done something to forfeit public esteem," she replied, with perfect coolness. "At present I trust my conduct needs no defence. Have you heard, by-the-bye, anything more of that terrible story about Mr. Ivor Lawrence. You knew him, I think, rather well?"

"Yes, I did," Grace replied, flaming up, and looking straight into her antagonist's eyes. "I knew him to be an honourable man, utterly incapable of the meanness of which he is accused!"

"You think so? I hope you may not be mistaken; but I fear there is no doubt of his guilt. It is only another instance of human frailty!"

"The worst human frailty is repeating and believing such falsehoods!" returned the girl, in a voice tremulous with indignation.

"We *all* knew him rather well," Mordaunt called out from the other end of the table, coming, like a gallant gentleman as he was, to his sister's rescue. "We are sure he will be proved innocent of the charge, but, in the meantime, we avoid the subject, don't you know."

"I can quite understand *that*," replied Lady Clydesdale, with a very peculiar inflection. "It is so very difficult sometimes to speak the truth about—one's friends. He was no friend of mine—so I can do it."

"We shall find no difficulty in doing that about you, Lady Clydesdale. I know you are truth itself, and you will supply us with all the details."

Mrs. Reid, who saw that the relations between her English guests were strained, here swooped down upon the young man, while her son, at the other end of the table, diverted Lady Clydesdale's attention to the congenial subject of Female Suffrage.

. . . . .

After dinner, in the drawing-room, Miss Pie came and sat beside Grace.

"I admired you so much standing up for your friends at dinner—Mrs. Courtly and that Englishman. Lady Clydesdale is a very able woman—quite a pioneer for our sex; but she is a little apt to lay down the law."

"It would be a bad thing if the law was what she lays down—I think she is more likely to do harm than good to any cause she sustains."

"My! I am afraid you are not very advanced, Miss Ballinger," said the little lady, with a twinkling eye. "Here we have to keep going all the time, or we get unhooked, and the train goes on without us. Lady Clydesdale is a powerful engine. Some of her opinions, from a member of the British aristocracy, have been an eye-opener to us. But we of the Press, of course, are bound to catch on, and support her in her levelling views—whether we quite believe them or not," she added, laughing.

"In some ways, you seem to be more 'respecters of persons' than we," said Grace. "If the 'level' you preach is the broad humanity level, irrespective of wealth, or brains, or race, how are you going to reconcile your attitude towards negroes, whom you will not associate with, nor even allow to sit down at a public table with you?"

"Well, there *are* reasons for *that*," returned Miss Pie, nodding her cropped head vigorously. "But apart from other considerations, the prejudices of race are not to be argued about. They may be just as irrational as the repugnance some people have to snakes, some to cats, some to spiders. But you were asking what 'level' we preach. Why, the level of success and prosperity, to be sure! We say one man is as good as another, if he is only successful; and if we educate the poor, and fire them with ambition, why should not everyone be prosperous? Why should there be those terrible inequalities of fortune?"

"Unless you can establish an equality of brain, of physical strength and energy, how is it possible that all men shall be equal? It was never so from the beginning of time. Were Cain and Abel equal? Your country being comparatively new, there is a greater demand for labourers in every field—a greater space for labour. It is not so with us; it will not be so with you, some day. And to my thinking, Lady Clydesdale's socialistic doctrines are calculated to make people dissatisfied with 'that state of life unto which it hath pleased God to call' them."

The little lady rubbed her hands, and laughed.

"I am quite satisfied with mine—especially to-night. It has been real nice to have a talk with you, Miss Ballinger. We get into such a groove of thinking! You take one right off the line, back into the tracks of the Old World."

And then some man came up, and the conversation ended.

CHAPTER VII.

The morning after this dinner, Mordaunt, looking up from his newspaper, said with a laugh,—

"Well! You've done it this time, Gracey—you profited by experience, and were civil to that jolly little woman who sat next me at dinner. I didn't know she was a Press writer till we were well through, but we got on like a house a-fire, and here is your reward and mine."

Then he read aloud :—

" Mrs. Reid offered a dinner at her sumptuous residence in Commonwealth Avenue, last night, to the Countess of Clydesdale, Sir Mordaunt Ballinger, Bart., M.P., Miss Ballinger, and Mrs. Frampton. Some of our most prominent citizens were invited to meet the distinguished guests, and especial interest was felt in the presence of the son and daughter of an Englishman who was so firm a friend to America, and so honoured here as the late Sir Henry Ballinger. Of the Countess, that advanced thinker, who recently addressed a large audience on Woman's Rights, it is needless to speak. Mrs. Frampton, Sir Mordaunt's aunt, is an elderly lady, evidently of great bodily and mental activity. The present baronet, like his father, is a Conservative in politics, and has the stalwart bearing and aristocratic air that we associate with the heroes of modern English romance. He is eager to acquire knowledge as to the natural resources of our country, and the urbanity of his manner and his brilliant social qualities " ("ho! ho!") "must make him welcome wherever he goes. As to his sister, the accounts which had reached us of her beauty and charm do scant justice to this fascinating English belle, who is not only lovely to a fault, but can be impassioned in her eloquence when roused, and combines acuteness of intellect with the frankness of a child."

"Well done!" cried Mrs. Frampton. "You owe Lady Clydesdale something for having brought out your 'impassioned eloquence,' Gracey!"

Then, seeing that her niece looked annoyed,

while a flush mounted to the roots of the girl's hair, she felt it was unwise to have alluded to that scene, and tried to change the subject. But Grace, with a resolute disregard to pain, said presently,—

"It was very nice of you, Mordy, to speak up as you did last night, feeling as you do on —the subject. I am ashamed to have been so roused, Aunty. I am ashamed to think such a woman could have it in her power to make me show what I felt. Passion should not be wasted on donkeys—even on malevolent donkeys. This one tries to knock you down, and ride over you. If she can find out where your heart is, she will plant her hoofs there. If not, she will kick at your brains. Nothing shall induce me ever to speak to her again."

Her aunt and brother exchanged glances, but no word passed; and presently Mordaunt began discussing financial matters with Mrs. Frampton, and expressing his intention of pushing on to Colorado as soon as possible. The relative merits of ranches, mines, and building property could only be investigated on the spot.

Grace had her own ideas as to what lay at

the bottom of this increased alacrity to go West, but she held her peace.

Mrs. Courtly was to take them to the theatre that night, and to return to Brackley the following day. Mordaunt declared that the chief attraction of Boston for him would then be gone, and he proposed to start for Chicago the same morning.

Will either of the three ever forget that evening, when they witnessed Jefferson's performance in "The Heir at Law"? It will always live as an epoch in their dramatic experiences. His "Rip Van Winkle" is not a greater triumph, though in a different line; for the exquisite naturalness of this fine artist transforms an artificial and farcical impossibility into an eccentric character of flesh and blood, in which he persuades us to believe so implicitly, that we should never be surprised to meet Dr. Pangloss walking down Beacon Street or Piccadilly. What a lesson to actors is here! The rigid fidelity to Nature—the nature of intonation, expression, and gesture—never allowing the laughter of the 'groundlings' to seduce him into exaggeration of any kind, this has its reward in our frank acceptance of, nay, our one sympathy with, a very unreal personage. Played by an inferior actor, I can imagine nothing more tedious than Dr. Pangloss would be, with his endless quotations, his facile venality, his outrageous wig. What seemed funny to our grandfathers does not amuse us very much. It needs the genius of a Jefferson to vivify the dry bones of an antiquated farce.

They all bade Mrs. Courtly good-bye with real regret.

"We must meet in Bayreuth next year," she said. "Will you give me a *rendezvous* for the end of July?"

"No," said Mrs. Frampton decidedly, before Grace could speak. "Before that, in my house in London. Make it your hotel, when you pass through, for as long as you can. Write or cable that you are coming; that is all that is necessary."

Grace had not felt so depressed since she landed in America, as she did during that journey to Chicago. It was in vain she said to herself, over and over again, that nothing which her aunt or Mordaunt, or, least of all, Lady Clydesdale had said concerning Ivor Lawrence, had the smallest effect on her. In one sense, it had not; she never doubted him. But the apprehension of an overwhelming trouble to him —a cloud, from which it might prove impossible to clear himself, had visibly strengthened in her mind. It was useless to argue against it; she could not shake off this cold, sickening dread, which swept in gusts over her. With her usual bravery she concealed her feelings; but, the call for social exertion being now over, there were long spaces of silence and solitude on the journey, when, with a book in her hand, she could brood over this trouble, unsuspected by her two companions.

The route chosen was by Philadephia. They did not stop at New York, but travelled straight through at night, arriving at their destination early in the morning. Here they halted the remainder of the day, and visited the "Hall of Independence," where the Declaration was signed, and where the room and its furniture remain much as they were on that famous day when the heat was so great and the flies so irritating that, as the assembled gentlemen flicked their silk stockings and wiped their brows, the voting is said to have been hurried through, and some members not even waited for. Yet the minority against the Declaration was a considerable one. As Mordaunt said to the amiable gentleman who acted as their guide,—

"Who knows how a cold day and a full hall might have changed the destinies of this continent, eh?"

The amiable gentleman, being a staunch patriot, looked confounded. Then, after they had been shown several pastels of the chief voters and orators of that stirring time, and had examined the building, which is like many a Georgian mansion in the home counties, and was built of red bricks brought from England, they were driven through some portion of the largest and most beautiful city park in the world. It extends over three thousand acres of hill and dale, wood and winding river, untortured by man. Happily, to use the guide-book's language, "Art has as yet done little for it." May it never do more. It is a beautiful spot, and Philadelphia may be proud in the possession of so unique a playground.

But what of its streets? Mrs. Frampton was greatly disconcerted by being nearly jolted off her seat as she drove along.

"Did you ever see anything like it?" she cried. "I thought New York and Boston bad enough, but this! How can the people who live in those nice little red houses, picked out with white marble, and marble steps, so beautifully clean—"

"Stoops. You must call them 'stoops,' Aunt," said Mordaunt.

"Stoops? I never heard of a stoup of anything but Burgundy—in Scott's novels. But never mind. I say, how *can* people living in houses that are like Dutch toys, so spick and span, tolerate such roadways? Really these Americans are an incomprehensible people!"

"No, not incomprehensible," said her nephew. "Ask any fellow here. He'll explain it fast enough. All public works are jobberies. If the streets were freshly paved to-morrow, in all these cities, it would be so badly done—so much money would be made *out* of them—that they would be as bad as ever next year."

"Abominable!" said Mrs. Frampton, with energy.

"Besides that," he continued, "this particular city is regarded by most Americans—especially New Yorkers—as 'a sleepy hollow.'

Miss Pie, who is a Philadelphian, told me she had been puzzled to see herself spoken of in some paper as the only female citizen who *suffered from insomnia*. Then she remembered the vile aspersion, which of course she denied. She was awfully good fun, that little woman. She gave me the idea of a middle-aged Puck, eh? Puck was a sexless sort of a being, I fancy."

The "Stratford" Hotel, where they stayed one night, met with great favour at Mrs. Frampton's hands; and so did the "Auditorium," at Chicago, in contradistinction to others on the road, which shall be nameless. The manner of serving every meal in the public room of these latter hostelries, all the dishes being pitched simultaneously in a semicircle of saucers round the consumer, was exasperating.

"Pray, do you expect me to devour fish, pudding, entrées, meat, and all those unknown vegetables at one and the same time? Why on earth can't you bring them separately?" she demanded of the astonished negro waiter.

Then the inevitable "pitcher" of iced water which came up each time she rang her bell, was another offence. She marvelled greatly as she looked down the long, crowded dining-room, and saw only this same iced water or tea being drunk at dinner by stalwart men. Any delusions, however, which she might have had as to their total abstinence were soon dispelled. Whenever she passed through the public hall, she saw some of these men at the bar; they were not then drinking tea or iced water.

The party stayed three days at Chicago, and were duly impressed with its vastness, the massiveness of the business portion of the city, the length and extraordinary diversity of architecture of its boulevards. Some of the least pretentious houses, and notably those by Richardson, were good, and gave a pleasant impression of happy home life, without ostentation. But many appeared to have been built regardless of any known principle, save that of endeavouring to out-do our neighbour. The classic and Gothic styles here take hands, and might almost be said to dance a *cancan* together, as they assuredly have never been seen to do before. These jokes in stone and marble of every hue are like a child's design for a palace, striking up spikes into the sky, and jumbling together turrets, and pillars, porticoes, and machicolated walls, in a fashion which Mordaunt declared entitled it to be called " the Porcine, or Bristle-on-end " style of architecture.

Of course he went to witness the assassination of the hogs, and, watch in hand, counted sixteen dispatched in one minute, while the ladies spent the morning at the Art Museum, and found, with wonder and delight, many of the gems of the Demidoff Collection, which they remembered in the Villa San Donato, at Florence. It seemed a curious illustration of the Chicago mind, munificent of everything but its time, and jealous for the city's reputation, that, while willing to expend large sums on such acquisitions as these, it had not leisure to arrange and exhibit them properly. Mrs. Frampton observed to a wealthy and acute citizen, to whom she brought a letter, that it was a pity such treasures were not seen to more advantage. His reply was characteristic :

" Well, you see, we business men are making money all the time. It is a race in which one is very soon left out of the running. If I go to

Europe for three months, I have to look pretty sharp to keep my place, I can tell you, when I return. Time enough to build galleries and all that, by-and-by."

This reminded Grace of a saying of Mr. Laffan's, "You must make the man before you can make the statue."

Mordaunt dined out each night, and was interested in meeting several of the shrewd business men who had amassed huge fortunes. He was almost tempted to invest in grain, live stock, or lumber,—but Mrs. Frampton, with a hand of iron, restrained him.

"Are you going to spend your life here?" she said. "These men do, and know what they are about. From their cradle they have heard nothing but money talked of. They are born 'cute men of business. What do you think that pretty child of five, in the hotel, said to me yesterday, when I asked him what he meant to be when he grew up. 'I guess I'll keep a store!' I expected him to say, 'I mean to be the President, or a general, or something.' But no, he would 'keep a store!' There you are. How can you compete with such people? No. Invest in something that doesn't require your constant personal supervision, or else leave it alone."

On one of these evenings there was a dance, to which all were bidden, but only Mordaunt went. He described the next morning how he had met a charming family, who all spoke of their "factory," which, on inquiry, he learnt was one of coffins! They referred in the most natural way to their industry; the father mentioning the "boom" there had been in his trade not long since, owing to the influenza, the son informing Mordaunt that he had charge of the brass nail and plate department; the daughter, that she designed the embroidery for the palls. This cheerful conversation took place in the intervals of the merry dance, and at the convivial supper-table.

"They were awfully nice," added Mordaunt, "but it sent cold water down my back, to hear them talk. It sounded like ghouls, fattening on graves." Then he told them of an old man he had met, who came from a neighbouring city, where he had amassed a vast fortune, and lived in great loneliness, his wife and children electing to reside in Europe. Why he had been weak enough originally to give in to this arrangement, was unexplained; but there was something at once humorous and pathetic in the monody of gratified vanity and personal loneliness with which he favoured the Englishman.

"I give you my word, I didn't know whether to congratulate or to condole with him," said Mordaunt, "when he told me that his only daughter was married to a French count, and that he should never see her again now, never! The tears trickled down his thin cheeks, as he said that she had forgotten all about her old home—her old father. But, in the midst of his trouble he recovered himself. There was balm in Gilead yet; 'You know, sir, *the family dates back from Charlemagne!*' So it is for this that such devoted parents are content to toil and moil, all their lives! By the Lord Harry! Self-sacrifice takes very funny forms, sometimes!"

And Aunt Su fully agreed with him.

Having heard from Mrs. Caldwell that she awaited their arrival, they started for Denver on the fourth morning; between which city and Colorado Springs her home was situated. Two days and nights travelling rather tried Mrs. Frampton's patience and powers of endurance, but the air, which grew keener and more elastic during the last twelve hours, as they left the plain and its vapours, and damp mists, and ascended the high table-land, surrounded by snowy mountains, invigorated all the party. Mordaunt declared his aunt was the youngest of the trio, when they alighted at the station, where Mrs. Caldwell's carriage awaited them. The beauty and strangeness of the scene—as they drove up a winding road, between rugged peaks of sand-stone, some nearly blood-red, others milk-white, others again like the root of amethyst, projected against the clear blue sky, and simulating the pinnacles, turrets, and spires of a castellated city—recalled the wild creations of Gustave Doré. It seemed too fantastic to be real. The very pine-trees looked tormented, springing from clefts in the rock, some erect, some twisted by the winds, but all with arms flung out over wide-mouthed chasms, where the eagles had their nests. The house stood high up on a shelf of rock, protected from the north and east winds, but open to the south. A slope of terraced garden lay below it, ending in a brook, which fell with the noise of tumbling waters, down a cañon at the back of the house.

"The Falcon's Nest," as it was called, built by the late Mr. Caldwell, was of wood, unpretentious, and in perfect taste, for its position, and the lives its inhabitants were meant to, and did actually, live. Labour and repose for some; comfort and hospitality for all who entered its broad portals, and found a pleasantly-diffused, but not oppressive warmth, reigning through the suite of rooms panelled with pine, where plenty of books, sofas, and rocking-chairs, invited the inmates to rest and be thankful.

Mrs. Caldwell and Doreen met their guests in the hall, to which the horns of buffalo and elk, and some magnificent bear-skins, lent a pleasant touch of savagery. Pierce Caldwell was at his office, and would not return till the evening. Alan Brown and another young man staying there were gone to skate; and after luncheon, Mordaunt, under Doreen's guidance, set off in a sleigh to join them. It was very cold, that still, dry cold, of which one does not realize the intensity until one consults the thermometer; but here, with a blazing wood fire to warm one spiritually, and hot-water pipes to perform the work practically, Mrs. Frampton declared the temperature was delightful; and her critical nature was pleased with her hostess's manner.

"That is a nice woman," she said to her niece, when they were alone, later in the day. "She doesn't 'protest too much.' She is sensible, well-bred, and knows just how much to say, and what to leave unsaid. All Americans have not that tact."

"Nor all English people either; I like that little Doreen so much. She is a sweet little thing; and the son, I am sure you will fall in love with the son, Aunt."

Mrs. Frampton's unspoken reply was, "I almost wish *you* would. Not seriously, of course, but just to distract your thoughts."

Pierce Caldwell returned at dusk, and found the ladies at tea. His frank charm of manner, even more than his good looks, won Mrs. Frampton at once; and knowing how energetic he was in the work he was carrying on, she began questioning him about it. Her capacity for taking a vivid interest in the details of other people's affairs, always distinguished her. It is not a common gift, that power of throwing oneself heartily into matters that do not personally concern one.

"Your mother tells me you have had a hard fight with your mine, Mr. Caldwell; but you have triumphed over all your difficulties?"

"Oh! mother exaggerates the difficulties. It only wanted a little patience. The mine when father died, you see, was a mere prospect. I had to develop it. It turned out much better than even father ever expected; but I had to go on with the exploration for two years before I thought it prudent to erect a mill."

"Well? And now," she continued, with eagerness, "it is proving a great success? Everything has prospered with you?"

"Yes," he said quietly. "Everything, up to the present, has prospered, I am glad to say. I am now going to turn it into a company. We have to erect other works, and it is too great an undertaking for one man, alone. Of course I shall retain a very large interest in, and the chief management of the company, but I can't work it all by myself."

"Humph!" said Mrs. Frampton, reflectively. "I suppose you want to get away occasionally, and amuse yourself in New York, like other young men of your age?"

"Well, no; I *do* go away, now and again,

when business takes me to New York, or Washington, but I don't stay much longer than I can help. I always feel as if things couldn't get on without me at the mines, and I love this place. I believe I am never so happy anywhere as here."

The skaters, with Mordaunt and Doreen, now entered. Alan Brown did not look happy. Doreen had driven the Englishman in her sleigh, to and from the rink; and Alan's proclivities for all that was English did not extend to a baronet, six foot high, who was notorious as a flirt, and who seemed inclined to try his hand —just to keep it in—upon the object of the young American's affections. In this he was quite mistaken; Mordaunt had the same manner with every woman under—and some over—fifty; which accounted for his being so popular. The unsophisticated Doreen thought him charming; and he was quite willing to be thought so. It gave him but little trouble to be nice to this bread-and-butter miss, whom he found really not so dull as he had anticipated. Alan only saw the effect, however, the young girl's increased animation and volubility, and he was proportionately depressed.

The other man, Bloxsome by name, was a Californian. He was not attractive either in appearance or manner to our friends, and as he only stayed one day at the "Falcon's Nest," it would be unnecessary, but for subsequent events, to name him here. How did he come to be a friend of the family? His manner and the tone of his mind contrasted so strongly with Pierce Caldwell's, that it was difficult to account for their apparent intimacy. He was coarse and loud, with a grating voice and accent, and his "spread-eagleism" was especially offensive to Mordaunt. To the ladies this was simply amusing. They did not in the least object to his thinking everything in his own country, beginning with himself, nobler, greater, and better, than the rest of the universe. It was a failing with which they were not wholly unacquainted in England. But foibles, which may be pardoned when allied with good manners, are more trying when accentuated with ill-breeding.

He sat on one side of Grace at dinner that first evening, and in the course of it—apparently accidentally—Miss Planter's name was mentioned. When Grace thought afterwards over what had passed, she felt sure that the accident was only apparent. Mr. Bloxsome had adroitly led the conversation up to the point when Grace's hand was forced, so to speak, and the "belle's" name dropped from her. He seized it.

"Clare Planter? Why, I know her quite well. I heard your brother was *vurry* intimate with her. Is that so?"

"My brother and I stayed in a country-house with her. That is the way of becoming intimate—if people like each other. And we both of us like Miss Planter."

"I reckon that's because she thinks such a heap of England and English people."

"Not entirely," replied Grace, coolly. "Of course we should not like her if she hated us."

"*We* find her ever so much spoilt since she crossed the ocean."

"Then she must have been very charming before."

"But Mrs. Planter is worse. She *is* a regular Anglomaniac. Won't call on anyone in Pittsburg now, I'm told. They are coming to Frisco in quite a few days. I guess you know that?"

"They spoke of the likelihood of going to California."

"Sir Mordaunt knows it is more than a 'likelihood,' I reckon. He will find Mr. Planter a stiff customer—not ready to come down with the oof, and not half as rich as he is supposed to be. Your brother is hunting around, I hear, for an Amurican heiress? Wull, you can just tell him this—no Amurican girl knows how rich she is till she can say, " Our Father, which art in Heaven."

Grace looked at him with a flashing eye, and there was ineffable scorn in her voice as she said,—

"My brother is not a fortune-hunter, nor did he feel impelled to ask Miss Planter to say her prayers."

Then she turned and addressed Pierce Caldwell on her other side.

She avoided Mr. Bloxsome as far as possible during the remainder of the evening.

CHAPTER VIII.

THE next day, when another slight fall of snow in the night had been frozen as hard as the surface of a wedding-cake over all the roads in the district, Mordaunt was driven by Pierce Caldwell in his sleigh up the beautiful drive his father had made along the mountain side to the mouth of the mine. Here he passed some hours in examining all the processes of silver-milling, and the many improvements, due to Pierce's energy, which had been effected in the works from the day they were established. He descended the mine by a new shaft opened a few days previously, which had been sunk several hundred feet, and which had laid bare fresh veins of ore, richer apparently than any which had yet been worked. Mordaunt's enthusiasm rose to fever pitch. When he had returned to the earth's surface, he gasped,—

"By Jove, Caldwell! this is the biggest thing out. You're a lucky chap—no! I suppose

I oughtn't to say that. How few young chaps would have been able to do what you have done! It is splendid—it really is!"

"Oh! it's no merit of mine. I have done nothing except just stick to the business, and watch, and let nothing slip. It is desperately interesting, I can tell you. And then the boys —they're a rough lot, but such good fellows. I'm fond of them all, and they'd go to—well! anywhere for me, I believe. This is the reading room I've built for them."

The "boys" were men, some well over fifty, begrimed with dirt, and many, it must be confessed, of forbidding aspect. The stories Mordaunt had been told of shots fired at random in saloons and drinking bars, gained in probability as he looked at them. Indeed, Pierce confirmed them from his own experiences as a youth, when he remembered, in a saloon, having to throw himself flat on the ground "to prevent stopping the balls," and the floor was strewn subsequently with wounded men. He repeated an anecdote of lynch law in those not-far-distant days, as he heard it, in the words of the narrator, "which," he continued with a laugh, "I think are characteristically succinct. The fellow was telling me how their camp had suffered from the robbery of horses, and he added, 'But I tell you, sir, that we collared a man the other day, *owning* a horse that didn't *belong* to him. The next thing that man found was that *his legs were not touching the ground!*"

Mordaunt laughed heartily at this graphic euphemism, and then said,—

"I suppose they are getting fast civilized now? All the Bret-Hartism will be swept away before long—eh?"

"Why, yes. We have schools now everywhere, and churches and institutes. They spring up like mushrooms."

"But who builds them? All along the track of the railway I saw big towns growing up. It seems little short of miraculous in so short a time."

"Well," said the young man, with an amused expression on his handsome face, "you see it is like this. There is a contractor who undertakes to build for each municipality. If they order fifty houses, he throws in a school. If they order a hundred, he throws in a church. It is as well to do the thing handsomely, for he is 'cute enough to know it is a remunerative advertisement."

The ladies now drove up in a *char-à-banc* with the other two men. Alan Brown, having had the field all to himself for some hours, looked reconciled to life, though he would have preferred life in Piccadilly with Doreen, to life under the same conditions in the Rocky Mountains. But the young girl had pacified him, I presume, as to the English baronet, and, indeed, Ballinger showed himself to be so entirely engrossed in the ninety-stamp dry-crushing silver mill, that there was no pretext for a renewal of the young American's jealousy. Mordaunt found an opportunity of whispering to his aunt,—

"This is the investment for me. I'm sure I can't do better than get all the shares I can in the new company that is being formed."

But Mrs. Frampton demurred.

"Don't be in a hurry. This climate is really too exciting to judge of anything dispassionately. Wait till we get damper, my dear. I am ready to jump out of my skin." Then, to Pierce, who came up at that moment, "Mr. Caldwell, how do you manage to exist, with your nerves in the constant state of tension they must be here? When your butler handed me potatoes last night, and touched my shoulder, I nearly screamed, he gave me such a shock. And I find I send out blue sparks every time I turn the brass handle of the door! It is frightful. I am become one vast electric battery!"

"You would no doubt be able to light the gas with your fingers. Some people have more electricity than others. I haven't so much, and get along here very well. And this dry climate has its advantages. We are going to lunch on the mountain side, if you are not afraid?"

"What! In the snow?—To be sure, the sun is very hot, and there is no cold wind—"

"Oh! yes, and we will find a sheltered place under the rocks. My mother and sister always do this when they come up here to lunch with me; for the men's saloon and reading room are not odoriferous. You won't find it cold, *al fresco*, such a still day as this."

Nor did they. Their luncheon spread upon the crisp snow, a cloudless sky above them, the sun pouring down on the little amphitheatre of rocks in which Pierce had ensconced the ladies, Mrs. Frampton declared it was an ideal midday dining-room—a combination of Davos-Platz and Cairo, which left nothing to be desired.

Bloxsome in his coarse loud way was amusing; but the instinctive dislike of our English friends seemed to be shared by Alan Brown, between whom and the elder American there was a constant sparring. Grace confessed to herself that the youth's Anglomania must be trying to one of his countryman's boastful temper, but this did not excuse the bad taste of Bloxsome's rejoinders. When Alan described, with boyish enthusiasm, a driving tour he had taken through the north of England, the other said,—

"Why do you squirm about English scenery so much? Say, can you find anything in all England to compare with this, I should like to know? Talk of their lakes! Why, they're mere ponds; and their rivers, ditches, beside ours."

"Size isn't everything," said Alan scornfully. "The lovely roadside hedges—the beautiful roads themselves—then, the dear old-fashioned inns, the ruined abbeys, the historic castles—what have we got to compare with *them?* Travelling here is beastly. No wonder Americans travel very little in their own country for pleasure."

Bloxsome gave a coarse laugh. "No, they transact their business at home, and go abroad for amusement. English people amuse themselves at home, and come here to invest their money, or pick up heiresses."

Pierce Caldwell blushed; and cut in with some wholly irrelevant remark, talking fast and laughing, in the impotent endeavour to obliterate the effect of this speech. And when Mrs. Caldwell found herself alone with Mrs. Frampton afterwards, she took occasion to say,—

"You must please forgive our unmannerly cousin. His education was very much neglected. He is a rough diamond."

Mrs. Frampton said, incisively, "He should be cut."

Mrs. Caldwell, not choosing to understand the *equivoque*, remarked that the world was the best lapidary in such a case; and John Bloxsome had seen little of any other worlds than those of San Francisco and Pittsburg.

"His father was one of my husband's greatest

friends. He died many years ago, and since then John comes and goes as he likes in our house. I wish I could give him better manners, poor fellow!'

Mrs. Frampton pursed her lips, and made no rejoinder. She felt such doubt as to the intrinsic value of the diamond, that silence was her only refuge.

Mordaunt, in the meantime, was impelled to say to Pierce,—

"That's a queer fellow, that Bloxsome! Is he always like that? or has he some special grudge against us?"

"He is not always like that. I can't tell what has come to him. I'm afraid the truth is he doesn't like anyone being more noticed than himself, especially an Englishman."

"What an ass! Where has the fellow lived all his life?"

"Oh! In a very narrow circle. Never was at a public school, or at college. Now he lives chiefly between San Francisco and Pittsburg."

Mordaunt whistled. "Ho! ho! I think I begin to understand. Is he well off?"

"Fairly so, I believe. But he never talks to

me of his affairs. I've known him ever since I can remember; but to say the truth, we have not much in common."

"So I should think. I like that young Brown much better, though he scowled at me awfully yesterday; but," he added, laughing, "I think to-day he has found out I am not such a bad chap after all."

No more was said; and as Bloxsome departed the next morning, he was soon forgotten by our friends. Mordaunt set off the same day for his old brother-officer's ranche, not more than a hundred miles distant, whence he was to visit Pueblo, leaving his aunt and sister at "Falcon's Nest" for a week.

It was a pleasant, tranquil one to the small party, reinforced once or twice by visitors from Denver or Colorado Springs. But towards the end of that time, Grace watched eagerly for the arrival of each post. She counted the days, the chances of delays, and accidents; it was just possible during the three weeks which had elapsed since she wrote to Ivor Lawrence, for an answer to have reached her. But none came. His name was never mentioned between her aunt and herself; and she had so schooled herself, as not to betray the anxiety she felt. Mrs. Frampton was of course ignorant that her niece had written to Lawrence; and did not suspect the torture of "hope deferred" which Grace suffered.

She rambled alone up the cañon sometimes, when she could slip out of the house unperceived by Doreen, who was generally her companion; and sitting down there among the rocks, her face dropped its mask, and her heart called aloud to the one man on earth for whom she felt she would make any sacrifice. Yes, though "the world" should henceforward eject him from its portals, and brand him with infamy, though her kindred should refuse to receive one stained with so deep a dye, would she hesitate to go to him, to share his obloquy, if only he would come to her with open arms and say, "You have believed in me hitherto; will you continue to believe in me, till death us do part?"

It was strange he should not write. Common courtesy demanded that he should answer her letter. It was true she had given him no address; but he must have known that anything sent to her home would be forwarded.

But perhaps he was waiting to do so till he could tell her the result of the trial. She rarely saw an English newspaper. Mordaunt had one sent him, but it arrived very irregularly; and, whether intentionally or not, he generally kept it to himself, or took it to his aunt's room, to discuss the Financial article. But now he was gone, and his papers were sent after him; and any chance of learning a decision in the law courts was at an end.

He wrote from his friend's ranche, fairly pleased with the life. "Charrington is doing very well; and if a man sets himself, body and soul, to work here, on this gigantic farming scale, he may make a good thing of it. If I married, and gave up English politics, and was content to lead a purely pastoral life, I am sure I could make it answer. But Charrington advises me strongly not to invest money in a ranche, unless I am prepared to devote myself to raising cattle, and so on. It is an awfully jolly life for a short time; I feel as fit as a four-year-old, but I fancy it would pall after a bit."

Then, from Pueblo, a few days later, he wrote :—

"'Real Estate' in Pueblo! After all, *that* I believe is the investment that is the most absolutely certain of bringing in very large returns ultimately; for mines are always uncertain, are they not? And railways fluctuate. But in a rising city like this, land *must* increase rapidly in value, year by year. What do you say?"

"I say," wrote his aunt in reply, "that I can't trust my own judgment here, far less yours, my dear Mordaunt. All these speculations look so lovely on the spot, that one must get at a little distance from them to judge if they stand upright, and are as solid as they seem. I trust Pierce Caldwell implicitly; he is a fine fellow and a clever fellow, and he has done splendidly so far. But he is young, and naturally sanguine. Leave his mine and your Pueblo building speculation alone for the present. There can be no harm in a few weeks' delay."

And this advice was enforced, with strong verbal exhortation, when her nephew, drifted hither and thither by the contrary winds of transient enthusiasm, returned to the bosom of his family, and held counsel with his aunt.

But such counsel was not possible on the night of his arrival, which was coincident with the unexpected appearance of an omnibus full of young folks from Colorado Springs. This "surprise party" brought a fiddler with them, and were greeted by Mrs. Caldwell with a cordiality which indicated unbounded confidence in the resources of her larder. Mrs. Frampton stood aghast. She thought with what consternation the head of an ordinary household in England would view the inroad of a dozen hungry young men and women, prepared to make a night of it, and, if heavy snow should prevent their departure, by no means indisposed to pass two or three under their friends' hospitable roof! Happily, in this case, the snow did not descend till they were gone, when it effectually blocked the mountain roads, and the railways, delaying the Ballingers' departure two days. But this night, though dark and windy, was fine, and the heavily laden omnibus with its four horses performed the journey to and fro in safety, depositing its hilarious freight at their respective homes in the dawn of the winter morning.

To the elder Englishwoman, accustomed to

the undemonstrative enjoyment of her own country-folk, the boisterous high spirits of these young people, under no conventional restraints but those of propriety, were a revelation. "Could they really *all* be as much amused as that?" she asked. "And was it necessary to make such a noise about it?" Grace declared that a pleasuring in the days of Queen Bess might have been on this wise, but not later, in England; not when the corrupt manners of the Stuarts, and the buckram and whalebones of the House of Hanover had rendered impossible all frank demonstrations of joyousness among persons "of quality." With what shouts of laughter these young Americans arrived! With what security they claimed their welcome! Did ever the finest stroke of art arouse such tempests of hilarity as did this small and well-worn joke of the "surprise"? They danced with the vigour of Highlanders at a Northern Meeting. Mordaunt, of course, led out all the girls in turn, and Grace, though with no heart for capering, if the truth had been known, waltzed with most of the young men.

For this act of self-sacrifice, let us think she

had her reward, when, on the arrival of the post, a few hours before the Ballingers were to leave the "Falcon's Nest," a thick packet was placed in her hand.

How she blessed that forty-eight hours' detention by the fall of snow! But for it, she would not have received this letter, which had been already delayed in transit, for many days. She hurried to her room and tore it open. It was a long document, extending over many pages, and this is what she read :—

CHAPTER IX.

"King's Bench Walk,
"February 28th.

"My dear Miss Ballinger,—I thank you heartily for your letter. It has brought the only great pleasure I have had for months. This has been a miserable time; but I hope and believe it is nearly over. Your letter is the first ray of pure light that has reached me; I hail it as the dawn succeeding the black clouds that have overshadowed me, and hidden you from my sight. You will say the dawn might have broken sooner, that I have wilfully deprived myself of that light, which, had I looked, I should have seen on the horizon. That is true; and you who know me so well—better than any one, I believe—know my answer. I was too proud to go to you while this matter was pending, too sensitive as to what the world might say (and in that word I include your nearest relations), to appeal to you, to enlist your sympathy, to do aught which should force you into the position of my partisan. You have written; and my conscience is now clear in answering you. If I do so at some length, telling you my 'plain, unvarnished tale,' though it would seem tedious to many, I do not fear its seeming so to you.

"You have known me only as a poor, a very poor, man, struggling to make his livelihood, without influence, without prospects. My eccentric bachelor uncle, Mr. Tracy, my mother's brother, never gave me anything beyond a ten-pound note at Christmas. For many years I had every reason to believe that he rather disliked me than otherwise. I never sought him; I had certainly no expectation of his leaving me more than, possibly, a small legacy. His other nephew, my first cousin, Giles Tracy, was generally regarded as his heir; and, but for his conduct, I have no doubt he would have continued to be so, as he unquestionably was a few years since.

"It is just four winters ago that I received what I should call a peremptory request, rather than an invitation, to go down to my uncle at once. I obeyed the mandate, and found him in a state of great exasperation. His solicitor, Mr. Eagles, was with him, and remained in the room all the time I was there. I little thought of what importance his presence might prove to me hereafter! Giles Tracy had been gambling, and had lost heavily at Monte Carlo. He had not ventured to apply to his uncle to pay his debts, knowing, in the first place, that he would be refused, and secondly, that his prospects for the future might be seriously impaired with the crotchety old man. But a rumour had reached Mr. Tracy's ears, by some means or other—I never discovered how—that Giles had been to the Jews, and had borrowed largely at usurious interest, giving promissory notes, payable when he should inherit his uncle's fortune. It was to discover the truth in this matter that he sent for me. He expected me to ferret out the facts and report them to him. I refused to do so. He then got very angry, and said he would leave all his money to a hospital. I said he could do what he liked with his money; it was no business of mine, but he must take some other means of learning the nature of my cousin's monetary transactions. Giles and I had never been cordial friends, but I was not going to play the part of a detective towards him. And with that, as my uncle now turned the vials of his wrath upon me, I left Mr. Tracy's house. I did not see him again for some time; but I have reason to believe that this—which was the only conduct any honourable man could pursue under the circumstances—far from alienating my uncle, was the real cause of his conceiving more regard for me. It was then he made the only other will that has been found; wherein he divided his property between me and my cousin. I had from him, in the course of the following summer, a note begging me to go to Tracy Manor, and during the last three years of his life I paid him several flying visits. Giles' name was rarely mentioned on these occasions; but he said once, looking at me in a marked manner, 'I have discovered all I wanted about that scamp, without your intervention.' What he had learnt concerning him I know not, but that he *did* learn something, very much to my cousin's disadvantage, subsequently to the occasion I have named, is certain, and will, I fear, come out at the trial.

"I often found Mr. Eagles with my uncle, and one day, about two years before he died, he said to me, in Mr. Eagles' presence, ' I have cut Giles out of my will entirely, and have left all my money, as I told you I should, to a hospital.' I remember his looking at me very searchingly, as though he wished to see what impression his words made on me, and I remember also, distinctly, my reply: ' That is too cruel a punishment for the folly of youth.' ' Folly ? ' cried my uncle. ' Do you call that folly, sir ? I tell you he is a scoundrel !' If Eagles is forthcoming at the trial, he will remember that scene as well as the former one ; he will recall my words and my uncle's.

"On my next visit to Tracy Manor, I heard incidentally that Eagles' health had broken down, and that he had gone to New Zealand. He did so little business in the country town where he resided, that to give it up was no loss. The loss was to Mr. Tracy, whose amusement it seems to have been constantly to make fresh wills, or add codicils to old ones. I have found any number of draughts and memoranda in the old gentleman's hand, but the will he *professed* to have made in the spring of 1888, leaving all his money to a hospital, is not forthcoming. I find notes of increasing donations to myself, beginning in January, 1886—the date of my refusal to comply with his wishes as regarded Giles. Then comes the will I have already named, made in 1887. But all this, of course is worth very little as evidence that I did not influence him; the only evidence of paramount importance is Eagles'. It was difficult to trace him at first, for he left no family in England, nor any address, being uncertain where he would go. But he has been found, and his evidence will have been taken on commission, I hope, if his health prevents his returning to England for the trial.

"The last time I saw my uncle, he was very ill. Though I did not know he was dying, I felt confident he would never really recover, and I therefore resolved to speak to him about Giles. I had some difficulty in approaching the subject, but I referred to the last occasion when he had mentioned my cousin's name to me, and I said I hoped he would reconsider his decision. 'No,' he replied, 'my will is made; Eagles is gone; I am not going to alter the last will he drew up, and which I signed eighteen months ago. I haven't altered my mind, in any respect, since then.' 'I am sorry to hear it,' I replied; 'whatever faults Giles may have committed—' 'Call them by their right name,' he interrupted testily; 'call them *sins.*' 'Well, then, whatever sins he has committed, he is young, he has, probably, a long life before him; you brought him up to believe he would be your heir. It is cruel to cut him off absolutely, and without any hope for the future.'

"I traversed the same ground over and over again; I left the old man no peace, and at length I induced him to allow me to wire for an old solicitor, named Pringle, whom Mr. Tracy knew something of, from London. He promised me to add a codicil to his last will, devising the sum of 20,000*l.* to his executors, on trust for his nephew, Giles Tracy, securing by this means that my cousin should not beggar himself by gambling. I did not remain in the room when he gave these instructions, for my uncle said he wished to be alone with Mr. Pringle; and he vouchsafed no hint of the main tenour of the will, which, I then firmly believed, devised the greater part of his fortune, as he had told me, to a hospital. Nor did I learn till his death, three months later, when this will was opened, that he had left the whole of his vast fortune, except this 20,000*l*., to me.

"Mr. Pringle predeceased my uncle; his testimony would have been valueless, on the main points, inasmuch as he did no more than add this codicil to the will which had been executed eighteen months before. But it would have gone to prove that Mr. Tracy obviously chose that I should be kept in ignorance of the disposition of his money. He ordered me from the room, as I have said, before Mr. Pringle opened the will, and read it to him, as the old lawyer told me afterwards, at my uncle's request; 'And his mind,' he added, 'was remarkably clear.'

"I have now shown you how false is the assertion that I brought a lawyer to my uncle's deathbed, to reverse his will in my favour. It had been signed and attested eighteen months before, without my having any knowledge of its provisions. As to the second signature, which my cousin was foolish enough, at first, to dispute, if proved to be a forgery, it would only affect his legacy of 20,000*l*.

"The world has been very ready to believe that I am a blackguard; therefore I have kept aloof, alike from friend and foes. I will neither conciliate the latter, nor oblige the former to declare themselves for me, until my name is cleared of this foul charge in the open Court of Law.

"When I heard I was my uncle's heir, my first Quixotic idea was to divide the fortune with Giles. That idea, of course, I soon dismissed, not alone on account of his attitude towards me, but because I felt I should not be justified in contravening my uncle's express wishes as regarded the fortune which his industry had built up. Could I think that Mr. Tracy had formed an unjust estimate of Giles's character, I can honestly say I would, even now, give him up half the estate, regardless of the misconstruction such an act would meet with from the good-natured world. But I have ascertained that my uncle had ample reason for deciding as he did. I say no more. The trial will come on in a few days. Everything in law is uncertain—except the costs! Eagles is due this week. If he dies on the passage, or that by other misadventure, his evidence is not forthcoming, I shall be bitterly, grievously disappointed. Not that it will affect the issue of the case; I know that my adversary cannot upset the will; he has not, legally, a leg to stand on. But between technical and moral victory, there is a wide difference. The attorney's testimony as to my uncle's anger against Giles, which led to his altering his will and sending for me, this, and his having been present at our interview, are of the utmost importance to *me*. Without this testimony I shall not feel that my character is completely cleared in the world's estimation. Is this over-sensitiveness? I do not think so; I am afraid you will. But at all events, whether I obtain this satisfaction or not, you will hear from me as soon as the trial is over. Until that time I must be silent; I can then, without fear of what man may say, ask you a question which I have not felt myself, hitherto, entitled to do.

"And so, my dear Miss Ballinger, for the present, farewell!

"Your very faithful friend,

"IVOR LAWRENCE."

The long strain was ended at last. Her joy found its vent in tears. What did anything signify now? Between the measured words, the self-imposed restraint, she read the truth— the truth which, she repeated to herself, over and over again, she had known all along. Grace fell on her knees, there, beside the window, where she read the letter, the window which looked out on the rocky peaks and snowy summits of that wonderful region, and thanked God, child-like, for her deliverance from the sorest grief it is given humanity to suffer— disillusion.

When she arose, there was a light on her countenance which shone there all day. But those who loved her, knowing nought of the letter, only said to each other,—

"How radiant Grace looks—quite like her old self. At last she is beginning to forget!"

They left that hospitable home, to which they will always look back with grateful and pleasurable recollection, the next morning. Except on the higher peaks, and in the fastnesses of rock, the snow was gone. There is no thaw in that blessed region; the snow is absorbed by evaporation, and the rich brown earth appears from beneath it, offering at once a solid resistance to the feet of man and beast.

The Caldwells accompanied them to the "depôt"—American for railway station—and there, while they were bidding the travellers good-bye, a head appeared at the window of a private car, which seemed to Mordaunt like a direct manifestation that Providence was actively employed on his behalf. How otherwise could it be accounted for—surely not by mere paltry coincidence,—that Mr. Planter should be travelling to San Francisco by this train, with his wife and daughter?

The greater part of the journey Mordaunt passed in that private car. Mrs. Frampton and Grace were also invited to take their seats in it, but they candidly confessed that they found it too fatiguing to talk all day long in a train, and confined themselves to paying a daily visit to the ladies at tea-time. At first, Grace had some a-do to persuade her aunt to receive this small hospitality, or, indeed, to be passably civil. She was extremely annoyed at meeting these people, "the only ones," as she said, "on the whole of this continent, I particularly wished to avoid." But she was too clever not to accept the logic of events. Since the girl and her parents were there—under her nose—the best thing she could do was to study them; not to put herself in the wrong with Mordy, and so damage her influence, by her demeanour to his friends. The father belonged to a type she had not yet met, and him she soon got to like. He had no pretension of any kind, but possessed great shrewdness, and considerable business capacity. Unfortunately, he had also an inveterate love of speculation. He had made three fortunes, and lost two. He spoke quite simply of his deficient education, his early struggles, his successes, and his failures. He was now on the top of the wave. But (Mrs. Frampton asked herself) how long would he remain there? As an acquaintance, she found him really quite interesting; he told her so much about railway-stocks, in which he had a large amount of capital, and explained to her the resources of the country, through which these lines passed. "But," as she said to her niece, "clever and straightforward as the man is—and he does impress me with a great sense of straightforwardness—one would never feel safe with such a speculator! He told me openly he didn't wish his daughter to marry an Englishman, and though he would never forbid her marrying anyone she loved, he would try and prevent it by all the weight of his influence. That is my only hope! I see Mordy is very far gone. But the girl does not care enough about him, I suspect, to oppose her father."

"Perhaps so. I am not sure. How do you like her? Don't you think, besides her beauty, that she is very attractive?"

"I am always attracted by beauty. You know it is a weakness of mine. And she has a nice voice and good manners. I won't say more at present. I must watch her. But if she were an angel straight from heaven, I shouldn't wish Mordy to marry a girl with such uncertain prospects."

Grace smiled.

"I suspect the angel straight from heaven would not come, 'in utter nakedness, but trailing clouds of glory!' Mr. Planter, who seems devoted to his daughter, would not allow her to be dependent on his speculative ventures, I should think. However, it is no use worrying about it, Aunty, one way or the other. The thing may never come to pass."

"No. Mordy suffers from chronic inflammation of the heart. Only he has the disease in rather a worse form than usual. I wish it had been Beatrice Hurlstone, however."

Her niece made no reply. It was wiser to let her aunt absorb and assimilate the Planter family slowly, than to cram them down her throat. And the next day Mrs. Frampton said,—

"I have been talking a good deal to the mother. I don't dislike her. She is not as clever, she has not the worldly tact, of Mrs. Hurlstone, and is evidently inferior to her daughter and to the husband, but I don't think she is a bad sort of woman."

"Certainly not. On the contrary, most amiable."

"She has been telling me a great deal about her girl's bringing up."

"Ah! That is a favourite subject of hers."

"She says they both prefer England to America."

"The daughter does not go that length, at present. Mr. Planter is a very indulgent husband and father, but I suppose he would not be pleased, if he heard his wife say that."

Mrs. Frampton complained much of the tedium of the journey, though the capacity of roaming through a long suite of cars, of visiting, when so minded, the one devoted to refreshment, and of studying the Planter family at stated intervals, broke the monotony of those three days and nights. To Grace, her head pressed against the window most of the time, with a wonderful panorama rolling past her dreamy eyes, the time did not seem long. Her thoughts and heart were far away; now, in some foggy chambers in the King's Bench Walk, now in the yet foggier law courts. Therefore it was that her eyes looked dreamy, though they gazed on the grand scenery of the "La Veta" range, till darkness swallowed it up, and though they opened at daybreak, to find those mountains lying, like a string of pink shells on the horizon, their bases still veiled in blue mists, while the tawny yellow prairie, and cliffs of sandstone in the foreground, were gradually being kissed into life by the rising sun. The whole of the journey was memorable for its beauty and strangeness, and will never be forgotten by that solitary watcher at the car-window, though it seemed at the time as though her mind were too much engrossed to be very sensitive to the impression of outward objects. Through the lovely plain of Utah, past Salt Lake City, surrounded by its still leafless gardens and orchards; over wild stretches of frozen prairie, when the little dogs come out of their holes, and sat up unafraid on their hind legs, to watch the train; down, at twilight, into the very heart of purple-folded hills, clear-cut against the orange glow of sunset; boring its way through mighty walls of granite, the train sped on; till the morning of the third day broke, and revealed a very different scene. It was as though a wizard's hand had touched the road-side, the vast stretches of garden and vineyard, with an emerald green, the vividness of which, no doubt, seemed greater by contrast with the mid-winter the travellers had been looking upon but a few hours since. Here, in California, it was not spring, but already early summer; arum-lilies thrust up their sheafs of bloom behind the palings of little white-faced houses; great fruit farms were a-flush with almond, peach, and apricot blossom, and here and there scarlet and gold flashed out among the greenery as the train rushed by.

To two young persons without much poetry in their composition, the one engrossed with his companion, the other pleased, amused, and flattered, these varying aspects of nature, and the sudden melting of the iron bands of winter, spoke only the driest prose. It had been cold; was now suddenly warm; instead of snow and ice, green blades of grass were sprouting everywhere. And that was all. Had they read, and if so, did they understand the sweet old fable of " The Sleeping Beauty," awoke by the magic horn of love? Certain it is, that the fancy of neither suggested any analogy between that fable, and the frost-bound earth, casting off her fetters, under the warm breath of spring, arising and putting forth her tender buds, and bursting, after slumberous silence, into song. And no doubt it was just as well. Had either been of an imaginative temperament, he or she would not have suited the other—for all present purposes—as well.

The third afternoon they passed the Golden Gate, and entered the fair city of San Francisco.

CHAPTER X.

Two young men were waiting at the "depôt," evidently prepared by telegram for Miss Planter's arrival. In the course of the evening several more appeared at the Palace Hotel; among them, Mr. Bloxsome. And during the Planters' stay at San Francisco, their rooms were scarcely ever free from her admirers, who came there, sometimes "single spies," sometimes in "battalions."

These half-dozen young men were, one and all, beginning with Freddy Bloxsome, unfavourable specimens of San Franciscan youth. One or two of them were handsome, one or two were apparently not ill-educated; but they had enjoyed few social advantages, they were loud and familiar; their standards of conduct were low, and they moved in a circumscribed orbit, outside which they neither knew nor cared for anything. Their attitude towards Mordaunt Ballinger was not openly inimical.

Civility, which would have been overpowering, but that it lacked the ring of sincerity, was the rule. They were always offering Mordaunt "drinks" at the bar, whenever he passed through the hall, or inviting him to go to a gambling saloon, or other haunt of virtue, all of which he rather loftily declined. Nor did they fare much better with Grace. She marvelled at Miss Planter's toleration. But early association, custom, and that wonderful adaptability of hers accounted for it, she supposed.

This only partially interfered with the intimacy which chance had done so much to forward between the Ballingers and the Planters by the fact of their travelling those three days together. Mrs. Frampton would certainly have declined the drives to the seal rocks, and the "Presidio," the theatre parties, and the expeditions by night to the "Chinese quarter," in which she and her niece joined, had her mind not been gradually inured to accept the idea of the Planters as of something which it was useless to try and avoid. And indeed, personally, she had no wish to avoid them. She was indisposed to accept the handsome American girl as a fitting wife for Mordaunt;

but, short of this, she liked her fairly well; and with *père* Planter she was now great friends. The mother and she had not much in common, and the young men annoyed her—perhaps too evidently. But, on the whole, there was no denying that the Planters, being in the same hotel, and being so cordially disposed towards the English trio, made their stay at San Francisco far more agreeable than it would otherwise have been. That this should be so in the case of Mordaunt was a foregone conclusion. Yet, strange to say, he was the one who seemed least happy. What his aunt called "the braying chorus," disturbed his equanimity even more than it did hers. His manner towards these noisy young men had, it must be confessed, that exasperating superiority which is calculated to inflame animosity more than anything else. Clare—perhaps of set purpose—was occasionally capricious in her demeanour towards him. As a rule, she certainly showed more preference for the society of her English admirer than for that of any other man. But, now and again she would, almost ostentatiously, choose Bloxsome, or one of the "braying chorus" to walk with, or retire to a corner of the room with, and converse with in whispers, to Mordaunt's utter distraction. He did his best not to let his wretchedness be seen at such times; but to his aunt and sister it was only too apparent. This irritation was further aggravated by the receipt of letters which he burned, without naming them, at the time; but the effect of which was apparent to both Mrs. Frampton and Grace. The former was not altogether displeased. If, by suffering, the evil she dreaded could be averted, why, then, it was better so. But each, after her own fashion, acknowledged the obligations they were all under to the Planters.

"They certainly are very kind," said Mrs. Frampton, "much kinder than English people would be to three Americans of whom they knew so little. And what surprises me is that Mr. Planter should not avoid us altogether, if he does not wish his daughter to marry Mordy. To *our* ideas, it seems very odd—letting a man be with your daughter so much, if you want to discourage him."

"That is because you do not understand the American character, and way of bringing up. Clare has never been controlled; she doesn't know what it means. She likes Mordy's devotion—up to a certain point; as she likes these other young men dangling after her. Whether it means more than this, as regards Mordy, I can't say. I doubt if she knows herself. She seems to me, every now and then, to be afraid; to be determined to make a stand; not to be hurried, and therefore to go on as she does with the others."

"I am very glad she does," said her aunt decisively. "I like the girl, but she is an outrageous flirt; and Mordy's eyes had much better be open to the fact. All the same, it is not humanly possible she can prefer any of those creatures to Mordy, and therefore I can't understand the father letting them be so much together."

"I am quite sure opposition would do no good. If she were curbed, she would kick. Mr. Planter shows his wisdom in giving her her head."

"What a horsey illustration, my dear! What you say makes me feel more and more that the girl, attractive as she is—and I really *do* like her now—is not fitted for English domestic life. A woman who doesn't know what yielding means, and who wants a chorus of idiots, or of vulgarians like Mr. Bloxsome round her—is not our ideal of a wife."

"She would be quite different when she married, aunt. That is the peculiarity of these Americans. They take their fun out, as girls. When the serious business of life begins, and they are put into double harness—I declare I am getting horsey again!—they give up kicking, and rearing, and settle down into a steady trot."

"Well. I shall never understand them—never! How a girl who knows what an English gentleman is like, can for a moment tolerate such a set of men as I see round her! It passes all belief. How long does Mordy mean to stay here? As to business, it is all nonsense. He has left none of the introductions to business men, which he brought. The sooner we can get him away, the better."

"It will not make much difference. We are to go to Monterey and so are the Planters."

Mrs. Frampton gave a gesture of impatience. "Do they do it on purpose?"

"No. Mordy does it on purpose. I knew it all along. But we are powerless, Aunty.

There is nothing for it but to yield with a good grace. If this thing is to be, it will be, and we must make the best of it. Neither Mr. Planter nor you will be able to prevent it. But I don't feel at all sure that the girl means to marry him."

" I hope to Heavens she doesn't ! " ejaculated her aunt ; and at the same moment Mordaunt entered, with an open letter in his hand.

" This is the third blackguard anonymous letter I have received about the Planters," he said, as he pitched it into the fire. " Of course it doesn't affect me one way or another. It is curious the writer should think an Englishman would pay any attention to such cowardly attacks on his friends. I should like to tell old Planter, but of course, it's better not." Then he poked fiercely at the fire. There was a pause. Neither his aunt nor Grace chose to ask what the letters contained. But, after a moment, Mrs. Frampton said,—

" When are you going on to Monterey ? Soon I hope ? "

" Well, the Planters talk of going next week, I thought, if you don't mind, we might as well wait, and travel down with them."

"Why not go before them? I don't like arriving and departing together like a travelling troupe. And I don't like your being herded with all those men who crowd round Miss Planter. It is not dignified. You had far better leave the young lady a few days' uninterrupted enjoyment of her Californian admirers."

Mordaunt winced. "Miss Planter cares nothing for them or their admiration, I am sure. She has known many of them since she was a child. It is their way. It seems odd to you, Aunt, but it means nothing."

"Oh! I don't pretend to understand their ways, only I don't admire them, that is all. And I particularly dislike your being mixed up with men who are as likely as not to pick a quarrel with you. They are all jealous of you. Under their smiling manner I can see that. That dreadful Bloxsome is the only one who has the courage to be downright rude. If you take my advice, you will not prolong the situation."

Mordaunt took one or two turns through the room. "Do you think one of those fellows can have written this letter?"

"How can I tell? I should think it not unlikely. I imagine from what you say it must be written by someone whose object it is to detach you from your friends. And certainly nothing that any of those men did would surprise me."

By an odd coincidence that same evening, as Mrs. Frampton sat in close confab with Mr. Planter, while the young people, under Mrs. Planter's chaperonage, were gone to the theatre, the American drew from his pocket two letters, and said rather suddenly—

"Do you know a New-Yorker, named John Reid?"

"Yes; a very nice man. I knew him in Boston, where his mother lives."

"Is he a great friend of Sir Mordaunt's?"

"I think he may be called so. They have not known each other very long, but Mr. Reid was very kind to my nephew in New York, and useful in giving him advice."

"They had no quarrel? You have no reason to suppose he would abuse your nephew?"

"Abuse Mordaunt? Good gracious! No. Why should he?"

"I don't know; only I have had a letter sent me purporting to come from him, and forwarded by an anonymous correspondent. In that letter, he says some very hard things of Sir Mordaunt. I like all that is open and fair, Mrs. Frampton. I don't much care about anonymous letters. But I get a lot of them, all the time."

"Oh! It is a common practice here, is it? My nephew had one about you to-day, which he threw into the fire at once, Mr. Planter. He has had several, I believe. Anyone who pays attention to an anonymous letter deserves to receive plenty, that is all I can say. But this other letter, abusing my nephew, is *not* anonymous, you say? If it pretends to be from Mr. Reid, it must be something worse."

"Yes. I strongly suspect from what you tell me, it is a forgery. There it is. You can show it to your nephew. If he thinks it worth while, he can wire to Reid."

She gave Mordaunt the letter on his return that night.

When he opened it, he was startled. The writing so closely resembled John Reid's, several of whose notes, referring to business matters, he had preserved, that it was difficult at first to pronounce this to be a forgery. He read it aloud to his aunt. There was no direction, nor indication as to whom the letter was addressed.

It ran thus:—

"DEAR GEORGE,—You ask for my opinion of the Englishman, Sir Mordaunt Ballinger, whom you say you believe is a friend of mine. He *was* a friend of mine, until I discovered that he was a scoundrel, who ought not to be received into any respectable American house. His character is too wellknown in his own country for him to have any chance of retrieving his broken fortunes there, by marrying an heiress. Therefore he has come here, laden with debt and dishonour, to try and induce some rich girl, for the sake of becoming 'My Lady' to marry him. On arrival, he first made up to Miss Hurlstone, but they soon saw that he was only a fortune-hunter, and showed him the door. Now I understand that he is pursuing Miss Planter. If you know the family, it would be but kind to warn them as to this Englishman's real character. He is a thorough profligate, and he has a contempt at heart for all that is American, which he tries to conceal. It would be a sad day for any of our nice girls, in which she became his wife.

"I am, dear George,
"Yours cordially,
"JOHN REID."

Mrs. Frampton was the first to speak.

"What do you mean to do? Wire at once?"

"Yes, for Mr. Planter's satisfaction, not mine. Of course I know Reid couldn't have written that. But of all the cowardly, damnable tricks—!"

"What did I tell you this morning? Some of these men, in their mad jealousy and envy, are capable of anything."

"I couldn't have believed it! I hope old Planter attached no weight to this precious communication?"

"No, or he would not have shown it to me. He suggested that it was a forgery, with a calmness which showed that he regarded it as an every-day occurrence."

And a forgery it proved to be. The reply

to Mordaunt's telegram came in these words :—

"*Have no correspondent named George. Have written no letter concerning you to any- one.*"

Mordaunt took it to Mr. Planter.

"Is there no means of tracing the perpetrator of this vile fraud?"

The American shook his head and smiled. "These lies are of no account with us, sir."

"So I should hope, but they are not the less disgraceful."

"I have thought it better to show the document to my daughter, sir. She is the person most concerned. It is but fair that she should judge whether what is here said of you is likely to be true."

"The only part she might possibly believe, is that about Miss Hurlstone. Well, it is a lie, Mr. Planter. She was the first pretty girl I saw in New York, and I flirted with her once or twice, as any fellow might. She was never anything to me, and, from the moment I saw your daughter, I never thought of any other girl. I have asked her to marry me, and she has refused. But I'm not discouraged.

I'm still in hopes of getting her to alter her mind, and—and of getting your consent, Mr. Planter."

"Well, sir, I will be frank with you. I let Clare do pretty much as she likes, and I have no objection to you, personally. You seem to me a straightforward sort of man, who are only a bit spoiled, I reckon, by the life you have led. I don't want my child to marry an Englishman, or any other sort of foreigner. She is the only thing I have got in the world, and I want her to settle right down here in America, near me and her mother, when she marries. There now, you have it plain. I like you better than the men who are fooling around here. But they don't amount to much. She would never have one of *them*. Our girls like amusing themselves; it don't mean anything. And if you come right along with us to Monterey, you must do it at your own risk, sir—as I told your aunt. You must not reproach Clare with having led you on, when she meant nothing. And she would never marry without my consent."

This was plain speaking, and it certainly was not encouraging. Mordaunt felt that to follow his aunt's suggestion, and precede the Planters to Monterey, was the only manly course, consistent with his resolve not to be deterred in his endeavour to win Clare Planter's affections. To continue to take part in "The Braying Chorus," could not be profitable and would certainly not be dignified. Mrs. Frampton received the announcement that they were to leave San Francisco the following day with a satisfaction which she was at no pains to conceal.

That afternoon he had the courage to avoid joining the Planter party, on the plea that he must go to some shops with his aunt and sister. So, leaving the lower streets, where the chief traffic of the city is, they climbed steep ways where the Chinese and Japanese dwell in colonies, and visited tea-houses, and joss-houses, and bought quaint toys and strange wares, unknown to Liberty and Co. And, afterwards, still toiling up, they reached the eminence, generally called "Nob Hill," crowned with structures that look like Genoese palaces, until one learns that what simulated marble is but painted wood. These residences of the wealthy merchants are all embowered in green. Flowers look out of every gate and doorway. As to the arum-lilies they grow like weeds, thrusting their white elongated faces through the fences of even the smallest houses; and wherever there is space to let them stretch their mighty plumes, palm-trees and yuccas stand between the windows and the dusty street.

The ladies returned to the hotel, pleased with their last ramble through the city, of which they had seen more that day than they had done during all their drives the previous week. But Mordaunt was silent and depressed. His self-confidence was shaken. Had he made any progress since they arrived at San Francisco ten days ago? He could not feel that he had.

Clare Planter came into their room at dusk, apparently in high spirits. She looked unusually well in a white tea-gown, with some crimson roses on her bosom.

"So I hear you go to Monterey to-morrow. What a shame to steal a march upon us! And what a shame not to have passed the last day here with us, Mrs. Frampton!" she exclaimed. "But you must really come in this evening. We are going to dance. Two or three girls are coming, and I have been to get a pianist. Don't shake your head—I am sure, Sir Mordaunt, you can persuade your aunt and sister to come, if you like."

"Thank you," he stammered, growing hot and cold as he spoke. "It's awfully good of you—but—as for myself, I—I promised to go to the Bohemian Club to-night. Some fellows asked me to supper there—"

"Oh!" she interrupted, with her sweetest smile, "Ask the 'fellows' to come to us—bring them along with you. You can't refuse me—now can he, Mrs. Frampton?"

"I should be ashamed of him if I didn't think he could resist temptation," laughed his aunt.

"You do not mean that you refuse me?" She turned her sweet smiling face to him.

"I am sorry I am engaged," he replied quickly, without looking at her. "You have so many men—so many more than ladies—you can't want me. My aunt and sister must answer for themselves."

She was so little used to contradiction that she seemed literally struck dumb. Who was this man, whom she regarded as her slave, that he dared resist her sovereign will and pleasure?

"Grace and I will look in to wish you good-bye, after dinner. But it is not 'good-bye' for long, I believe?" said Mrs. Frampton, in high good humour at Mordaunt's firmness. He was really behaving better than she expected.

"Perhaps—I don't know," responded Miss Planter, as she twirled the tassel that hung from her waist round her finger, and then untwirled it. "Some of my friends are going to Santa Barbara. Perhaps mam-ma may go there instead."

"Your father spoke very distinctly this morning of going to Monterey," said Mordaunt, flushing suddenly.

"Oh! yes; but pa-pa will always do as mam-ma and I ask him. That is the advantage of having an American husband. Englishmen are not like that, they can refuse anything!"

She stung him with one sharp look from her beautiful eyes, and with a little *au revoir* to the ladies, swept from the room.

"If they go to Santa Barbara, I shall follow them," said Mordaunt recklessly, as soon as the door was closed.

Grace looked up with a smile.

"They will not go to Santa Barbara."

CHAPTER XI.

IF anything could have raised Mordaunt's spirits that night, it would have been his supper with the joyous Bohemians ; listening to their banjos and bright choruses, and hearing the tales of the "high jinks" they hold in the neighbouring forests in spring-time. Many members of that genial club were charming enough to make him forget that they were fellow-townsmen of vulgarians like Bloxsome, but nothing could disperse the cloud that overshadowed him.

The girl had grown dearer to him every day, and yet she seemed further from him than ever. He would not blame her, still less would he have allowed anyone else to do so. Had she not said, only six weeks ago, that she did not like him well enough to marry? Except during those three days in the train together—those three unforgetable days—they had never been alone, as they then virtually were, and nothing had passed to justify him in the belief that her heart had softened. On the contrary, she seemed to have taken special pains to prevent his forming such an erroneous idea. She treated him only a little better than the other young men round her—just so much as to rouse their jealous animosity—not enough to distinguish him as the one she had chosen from all the world. Though he had defended her against his aunt's insinuations, as regarded " the braying chorus," he did not feel the less secretly hurt. Therefore it was that he was here at the Bohemian club to-night, instead of gliding round the Planters' sitting-room, with his arm round Clare's waist.

He did not see the Planters the following morning. Mrs. Frampton and Grace had wished them good-bye the previous evening, and they were off early with a large party to San Rafael. Before the Ballingers left San Francisco that day, the English post had arrived, bringing nearly a week's budget of letters and papers. There was food enough for the mind, and to spare, to last them that short journey.

Mordaunt and his aunt sat together at the end of the car, Grace by herself a little distance off. Her letters were not very interesting, but she had several papers which Mordy had handed to her; only the last issues he and his aunt were reading. The debates naturally claimed the young member's first attention; the Society journals, and Pall Mall Gazette gossip as naturally claimed Mrs. Frampton's.

"Look! Look here!" she whispered, suddenly, turning to her nephew, and pointing to a paragraph, "Do you see this? Have you looked at the law reports?"

Then he read the following:—

"The termination of the great will case yesterday is a triumph not only to Mr. Ivor Lawrence's personal friends, but to all lovers of fair play, who have declined to prejudge the case, and who have viewed with grave reprehension the disposition in society to believe the allegations recklessly brought against a gentleman who had always enjoyed an unblemished reputation. Mr. Ivor Lawrence has suffered most cruelly during the past eight months, and it is but just that the false accusations he has laboured under should recoil upon the head of Mr. Giles Tracy, who, without the smallest evidence, dared to bring these charges against his cousin. That the course of the trial brought to light certain facts not wholly creditable to the accuser was the penalty he paid for his rashness."

Mordaunt turned to the law report in the *Times*, and there read, at large, the collapse of the first day. It had been expected it would extend over several, but Mr. Eagles' testimony was so complete and crushing, that Giles Tracy's counsel had no choice but to withdraw. Unfortunately for him, this withdrawal was not before certain indelible stains had been left on the young man's character by the solicitor's evidence as to the cause which led to the estrangement between the testator and his favourite nephew, an estrangement which hardened into virulent aversion as time revealed, more and more, Giles' true character. At the period of Eagles' last interview with his client, he had no idea Mr. Tracy could ever be persuaded to add a codicil to his will, leaving Giles 20,000*l*. He felt sure that nothing but Mr. Lawrence's strong representations could have brought him to do this. Mr. Eagles had made no less than four wills for Mr. Tracy. He believed all had been destroyed but this last one, in which he left everything to Mr. Lawrence. Mr. Tracy did not wish this to be known; least of all by the nephew he resolved to make his heir. Hence his fiction about the hospital.

When Mordaunt had read rapidly the half-column which contained this report, and had handed it to Mrs. Frampton, he sat brooding until she had finished. The silence was broken by her saying,—

"H'm! It is most unfortunate!—I mean unfortunate *just now*, when one wants to distract her mind from the subject. The man has behaved disgracefully to *her*, at all events, and the sooner she forgets him the better."

"Yes, of course; that's all right. But I must show her the paper."

"I don't know what to say to that. She looks so much brighter lately. I hope she is beginning to forget. I watch her when she little thinks I am doing so, and I see a great change for the better. I am afraid this news will undo it all, by turning her thoughts again entirely upon this wretch, whom I hate and abominate—for he has been the only cause of real dissension between Gracey and me."

"Can't help that, aunty. She *must* know. There's no help for it. It's an awful bore. Confound it! everything seems to go wrong since we came to California!"

Then, with a sigh which appeared to have its birth in his boots, and went quivering up his frame, he rose and walked down the car, to where his sister sat.

"Look here, Gracey. Here's something you'll be glad to read. I don't like the fellow. I think he behaved like a cad, though I stuck up for him that night at Mrs. Reid's, just to please you. But, of course, I'm glad to know he is not a scoundrel."

Her eyes sparkling, her face a-flush with excitement, she had seized the paper from his hand, even while he spoke, and her eyes ran rapidly down the column to which he pointed. When she had done, a sweet smile played upon her lips. She leaned her head upon her brother's shoulder, and whispered,—

"I never doubted him about this, or—or anything else, dear. You must never abuse him again—never—*never*, Mordy. He is the soul of honour, and of all that is noble and high-minded. His very faults are grand faults. You will learn to see that soon, dear—you will, indeed. And so will aunty, when—when it all comes right."

The branching of wide-armed cypress trees, and the incense of sweet flowers was all they knew in the young moonlight, as they drove from the "depôt"—surely the most poetical railway-station in the world — through the pleasure-grounds of the wonderful hotel at Monterey. They alighted at the terrace of a huge, irregular building, and the next minute found themselves in a big hall, crowded with ladies, some in evening dress, some with hats and jackets ready to sally out into the moonlight, and men smoking, drinking coffee, reading telegrams, or gathered in knots round two or three of the most favoured ladies in rocking-chairs. Some of these were pretty, some, according to our ideas, very much over-dressed for the occasion; all seemed to be enjoying themselves thoroughly, and not to be afraid of showing that they were. Small children were running in and out between elderly gentlemen's legs. Young men were strolling in the corridors, looking at the billiard players through the open door, and stopping to chaff the knots of young girls, clinging to each other with the effusive affection born of twenty-four hours' acquaintance. Aged ladies had besique boards between them, but were interchanging remarks in high-pitched voices none the less. Aged men were discussing Mr. Blaine's projects, the World's Fair, and canned fruits with equal vehemence. The babel of tongues, from the piercing falsetto of childhood downwards, was deafening to the travellers as they entered, but the scene was so gay, so pervaded with *bonhomie*, that even Mrs. Frampton declared later that it was amusing,—" amusing to *watch*. It would be a delightful place for a deaf person to come to. So lively. And the drum of *their* ears would run no risk, you know."

In the morning, Grace looked out on the most lovely garden of its kind she had ever seen, with glimpses of a sapphire-coloured sea, between the red lilac stems of pines, and the gnarled boles of ilex. On the other side, a little lake, surrounded by palms and bamboos; in the foreground, beds of cineraria and sweet-smelling stock, with bunches of arums and lilies raising their white crests above the masses of rich colour. The fresh morning air came up laden with the first breath of the flowers. As soon as she was dressed, she went out and watched the Chinese gardeners at work on their borders of floral embroidery, and wandered through the winding groves, across the railway and over the sand-hills that slope to the beach, where she sat down awhile, and felt tranquilly happy. It was good that her happiness had come to her here, where there were no jarring elements; where no constant social effort was needed, where nature was so rich, so fragrant, so untroubled. She could not have nursed the peace at her heart so securely in those great cities; even the wild crags and snowy fastnesses of beautiful Colorado, much as she loved them, would have harmonized less with her present mood than did the white-lipped sea curling on the yellow sand, and the tranquil spaces of lofty shadow in the garden, upheld by the mighty columns of the Californian pines.

The only cloud in the sky that day—and she could not feel that it was one impenetrable to the sun—was her brother's gloom. He thought that he need make no exertion with his aunt and sister to assume a cheerfulness he did not feel; and he looked as miserable as a man who has not lost his appetite can look. Mrs. Frampton was much concerned. She tried to talk of investments, but failed to rouse his interest. He was clearly in a bad way, in a worse way than even she had suspected. She was thankful to have got him from San Francisco. But now that they had brought him away, what were they to do with him, without companions, without purpose, or occupation? As she watched him at breakfast, slowly consuming an egg, with the air of an early martyr, she felt at her wit's end what to do. However, they must not all three sit still; movement was better than inactivity. She wisely insisted on their going the famous "seventeen-mile drive," and taking luncheon with them. She gave him a French novel, and bade him supply himself with an unlimited amount of tobacco. She took for herself an eider-down cushion and a sketch-book. And, thus armed against ennui, if the drive should prove disappointing, they started.

Though they drove along those shores

repeatedly during the weeks they remained at Monterey, it never, perhaps, looked quite as beautiful as it did that morning. The sea was a wonderful colour, more like the iris, with which the pine wood they first drove through was carpeted, than anything else in nature. Above the pine-needles and these purple-blue irises rose bushes of pink berberis, until the road opened out upon a wide down, fringed with rocks overhanging the sea. To-day there was a west wind, which lashed it into white foam, not only against the cliffs, but far as the eye could reach. Presently they gained a group of island-rocks, two of which were literally covered with seals, whose roaring and strange plaintive cries were heard more than a mile off. On the summit of their home they lay dark and inert, sun-dried, and probably asleep.

Lower down they were sprawling and floundering about, of a pale dun colour, ever and anon plunging into the foaming waves, such a picture of innocent enjoyment that it was pleasant to know they were never molested. They only frequent certain portions of the coast, and considering that they deprive the fishermen there of a large portion of their spoil, it is creditable that the law which forbids them to be destroyed or disturbed is so rigidly respected.

Soon after leaving this interesting colony, our friends came upon that unique feature of this coast, the great cypress forest, which affronts the winds and waves, stretching out into the very sea itself, a sentinel now and again thrust forward upon some prominent crag, its strong grey arms lifted defiantly against the foam that breaks impotently over it. The "cypresses," as they are here called, closely resemble the cedars of Lebanon, and have no apparent relation to the columns of solid foliage we are used to associate with the name. Here and there the bleached skeletons of these mighty trees, silver-lighted in the sun, some still erect in death, some prone upon the sweet warm grass that crowns the pink-grey rock, tell with magic brilliancy against the broad sovereignty of impenetrable green that dominates the sea. As Grace beheld these gnarled trunks, and twisted branches, bearing their solemn crowns aloft, and immovable above the assaults of lightning and of wind till death uncrowns and unrobes them, she felt that this was the realm of Epic Poetry, the ocean-forest of imagination; a kingdom unrivalled upon earth for its majesty of colour and richness of suggestion.

And now they rounded point after point, and she cried aloud to her companions in her glee, and they responded, after their kind. The same elements formed fresh combinations at each turn; the rocks standing out like castles in the sea, the cypresses, a beleaguering army, now advancing, now retreating, their dead lying round them unmourned, slain in the mighty battle with the winds of heaven, where, after centuries of strife, they had fallen, and others had stepped forward from the ranks to take their place.

In one of these little bays they stopped the carriage, and unpacked their basket. And when they had all eaten, Mrs. Frampton sharpened her pencil and attacked the scene with characteristic vigour. She was not goin to be beaten by the convolutions of a few trees—and those American trees, too. Mordy smoke his pipe in silence, and fell asleep. Grace rose, and wandered down among the rocks.

Just after this another carriage drew up a

little distance off, from which a man alighted.
If not an Englishman, he was very like one.
In age he appeared to be near forty; strong,
somewhat broad, and not very tall. He could
not be said to be handsome, his upper lip, from
which the hair was ruthlessly cut, being too
long and straight. But he had fine fearless
eyes, and the brow was broad and massive.
His walk was full of decision, and, in his
Norfolk jacket and knickerbockers, he had the
look of a man who would never waver, never
turn back, nor give in, under any ordinary
strain, physical or mental. He stood still for
a moment taking in the scene; in the foreground Sir Mordaunt Ballinger, Bart. and M.P.,
asleep, with his head on an eider-down cushion;
not far off, Mrs. Frampton, spectacles on nose,
her attention riveted on that group of hoary
cypresses; the coachman beyond, devouring
the remains of the luncheon. Was there no
one else? No. His eye scoured the scene;
then, making up his mind that the person he
sought must be hidden from him by the underwood and rocks, he strode down, unobserved
by Mrs. Frampton, to the edge of the cliff.

She was sitting on a rock, sheltered by the

trees from the west wind, her eyes fixed on the purple sea, with its green stains, and white lips curled in anger against the pebbles on the shore below her, when she heard a rustle in the grass, the crackling of a twig, and, looking up, saw Ivor Lawrence before her.

He had been present so vividly to her mind's eye the moment before that she was scarcely startled. She caught her breath, her cheek turned pale, before the blood rushed violently back there; that was all, as she stammered out,—

"Mr. Lawrence! How wonderful!"

He took her hand in both his, and held it for a moment or two, before he sat down beside her.

"Yes, it is wonderful to meet you in such a spot after our long separation. I started immediately the trial was over; I had made all my preparations beforehand, and vowed that nothing should keep me a day."

"We only received the papers with the result of the trial yesterday."

"I came over in the boat that brought the mails. Had I known your address I should probably have been here before them. But I had to wait in New York, to learn from your bankers where you were." Then he leant forward, and looked yet more intently into her face. "You *knew* that I should come—and come at once, did you not?"

"I—thought you would—if you could—but, of course I couldn't feel sure." Then she added, with that burst of sunshine in her face, and that rare naturalness which belonged to her, "But, oh, how glad I am! How wonderful it is to see you here, after all these months—here, in this lovely spot, when I have been thinking of you in London fogs! Oh! that horrid trial! How thankful you must be it is over!"

"Yes—not that I had, latterly, any anxiety as to the result. From the moment I knew Eagles was alive, I knew I was safe. If Eagles had not turned up, some good-natured people might still have doubted me."

She looked at him with her quickly-flashing eye, and the colour mounted again to her cheek.

"No one who knew you—who *really* knew you—could ever have doubted, though the trial had gone against you, over and over again!"

"I like to hear you say that. You can't repeat it too often; it is worth all the fortunes —all the triumphs in the world to me; it means my whole happiness in life. You have never doubted, through my silence, that I loved you better than anything in the world? You understood how it was that I kept silent, till I could face your brother, your aunt, everyone, without the suspicion of a stain upon my name?"

"No; I have never doubted, in my inmost heart, though I blamed you," she said, and the tears now rained down over her cheeks. He threw his arms round her, and kissed them away.

"My darling! it was my great love for you —my desire that your name should not be bandied about in connection with mine, as long as this accusation hung over my head."

She smiled up at him through her tears, while her head lay upon his breast, and said, with a little gesture of negation,—

"Perfect love casteth out fear.'

*   *   *   *   *

Nearly an hour later, Mrs. Frampton, having finished her sketch, went in search of Grace. The sight which met her, when, after hunting about for some time, she reached the little cove of rocks where her niece and a man were seated, their heads very close together, nearly caused the good lady a fit. Grace—Grace, of all the girls in the world! She was thunderstruck.

She could hardly believe her eyes. The man's back was turned to her. She uttered a loud exclamation and dropped her parasol.

Grace sprang up, ran towards her aunt, and embraced her. At the same moment her companion turned, and Mrs. Frampton recognized in him the man she had been abusing for the last eight months.

It was an awkward moment for her, but she was equal to the emergency. She seized the situation at a glance; congratulated him on the result of the trial; reproached him roundly for his silence; and, if I may paraphrase the poet, " saying she would ne'er forgive, forgave him." How could she do otherwise? She was too clever a woman to stick to her small field-pieces, when she found they were only loaded with blank cartridge.

Mordaunt joined them soon afterwards, and behaved like a good fellow as he was, first of all, and a man of the world as he was, afterwards. He grasped with heartiness the hand of the man whom he knew now was to be his brother. And in the ruddy gold of waning day behind the dark columns of the trees, the four drove back to Monterey.

CHAPTER XII.

THREE days later, Mordaunt, who inquired at the office every morning, whether Mr. Planter's family was expected, learnt that the best suite of rooms was retained for that gentleman, who was expected to arrive from San Francisco the same afternoon. His watchful aunt detected the change in his glad face when he sat down to breakfast; and she guessed the cause.

They arrived, happily without followers; though Clare took pains to let it be known that " some of her friends " were coming to Monterey for the night on Sunday. She met the Englishman's fresh demonstration of delight at having her here to himself once more, as she always met such calls, with every outward token of pleasure and response. Did he delude himself? or was there even a touch of something more, something which had not been there, in her manner to him, hitherto? Be that as it may, she had no idea of not letting him know how much his conduct at San Francisco had displeased her. They were alone in the garden, the first morning after their arrival, when she said,—

"You were awfully cross and disagreeable at San Francisco, Sir Mordaunt. I am glad to see you are ever so much nicer here."

"Well, there was good reason for my being cross there."

"Because of my friends? No; *you* were not at all nice to *them*. That was the trouble."

"Not nice? I like that! Come, come, the worm will turn at last. I don't want to say anything nasty about your friends. But, be honest, confess that they insinuated every sort of villainy about me, behind my back, though they *were* so sugary to my face. You know as well as I do, that one of them wrote those anonymous letters."

"I know nothing of the kind."

"Then I do. The expressions in one of the letters I received are identically the same that—well, I won't say *who* used to my sister when speaking of you and your father. Of course I didn't care a brass farthing."

"No one does in San Francisco. People

get them all the time, and no one pays any heed to them. That was no excuse for your treating my friends *de haut en bas*, as you did. It was very rude of you—very rude to me. And then, that last night, when I begged you, I actually begged you, to come to us, and you refused! After all your protestations. I never heard of such a thing!"

"I protest nothing more than I feel; indeed, much less. It is because I *do* feel, that I can't stand that lot of cads, what my aunt calls 'braying' round you. If you prefer them, well, then you'd better say so, and I'll retire. I hope I have the pluck to take my licking like a man."

"I have no doubt you will, with perfect equanimity," she said, resentfully.

"Well, you remember what I told you at Brackley. I can't talk a lot of sentimental rubbish. It ain't in my line. If you send me about my business, I shall be awfully cut up. I shall never be quite that same fellow I was, again, I fancy. And if you told me to wait, I'd do it, if you thought you would get to care for me. But to make one of the crowd, and see you encouraging them; no, I can't, and I won't.

I'd rather take the first train to New York, and return to Europe at once."

"You are quite at liberty to do so. If you expect an American girl to give up her old friends at your dictation, you are mistaken."

"'Friends' is a convenient term. If they were your real friends, I'd try and make them mine. They want to be something more, and are in reality much less. I shouldn't blame them for admiring you, God knows, if they were true, honest fellows; but they are not. They are double-faced. They are humbugs."

"The fact is, you are jealous of them," she said, laughing.

"I am not such an ass as to be seriously jealous of any *one* of them; but I am jealous, as every Englishman is, of the girl he loves wasting her sweetness; stooping to encourage a lot of men he thinks in every way her inferiors."

"Dear me! Men are very troublesome," said Miss Planter, stooping to pick a rose, "and Englishmen are the worst of all. Freddy Bloxsome says—" Here she stopped short.

"What does Mr. Bloxsome say?"

"He says the English are the most arrogant nation on the face of the earth, and I am afraid he is right! You are awfully stuck up, you really are."

"Perhaps I am, as an Englishman. I am proud of being one. Not as myself, Mordaunt Ballinger. I have nothing to be stuck up about."

"No, indeed!" pursued the girl, relentlessly. 'You are very nice, of course, and all that. But there is nothing so wonderful about you."

"Nothing; except my love for you."

He said this with an earnestness unlike himself.

The girl laughed, but the colour deepened on her cheek, as she replied lightly,—

"Do you mean it is wonderful you should care for anyone? or wonderful that I should be the present object of your attention? I am told they change every month."

"I recognize Mr. Bloxsome there. What I meant was, that I never expected, that it was wonderful to find myself caring about any girl as I do about you."

Miss Planter turned away, and began humming "*La donna e mobile.*" But there was a curious expression on her face, an expression which he would probably have been incapable of reading had he seen it. It told of an internal struggle between the forces which are ever at war in such a woman's complex character.

"All my friends whom you abuse would give up anything for me."

"Would they? Try them. That's all!"

"While you would sacrifice nothing, not even your pride. Look at the other night!"

"You call it pride; I call it honesty. I won't take the hands of fellows I despise, men who *forge*, men who write lies about me to your father, and lies about your father to me. That's a sort of sacrifice you've no right to ask. I simply *can't* make it. If Bloxsome were to come here, I am afraid I should kick him. Ask any other sacrifice, and I'll make it; my English home, my seat in parliament, I'm afraid I'd give them all up, though I know it would be wrong, if you wished it. As to money, I don't want your father to give you a penny. I'm not rich but I have enough to support a wife. All I want is that you should care enough for me to give up those fellows for my sake."

She looked at him for a moment steadily. Then she said, with a flickering smile,—

"No. I am not going to give up all independence of action yet. But here is a buttonhole for you," and she gave him the rose she had just gathered.

Nevertheless the young lady sent off three telegrams that afternoon, couched in the same terms:

"Sorry cannot see you on Sunday. Shall be engaged all day."

Three weeks slid by; weeks all too brief for four out of the group of friends, two of whom had nearly reached the full of happiness, while two were in the crescent stage, nearing, day by day, the second quarter.

Clare Planter's conquest was a slow one; if indeed that may be called a conquest which is not as yet proclaimed. Mr. Planter's sudden decision to leave Monterey, unshaken, for once, by his wife's and daughter's supplications, was due, no doubt, to some indication on Clare's part that the Englishman was beginning to be not absolutely indifferent to her. As long as she encouraged a number of other admirers, her father was not alarmed. But when he learnt that, on one pretext or another, she had put some of them off on three successive

Sundays (the only day they could get away from business), when he saw that the Englishman had undisputed possession of the field, he grew uneasy. He spoke with great frankness to Mrs. Frampton.

"I am going to take my daughter right home. My wife doesn't like it, but I think it wiser. And I have refused to allow her and Clare to go to Europe this year. It is about the first time I ever refused them anything. You and I, Mrs. Frampton, are of one mind, I don't want my daughter to marry an' Englishman. You don't want your nephew to marry an American."

"Pardon me, Mr. Planter," she replied, with a boldness begotten of the occasion, "I have no objection to my nephew marrying an American; and if I had twenty objections, they would be of no avail with him, on this subject. I see that now. He has some regard for my opinion, but where his feelings are concerned he consults no one. They are very deeply concerned, I am afraid, in this case. He is not rich, and I should like him to marry a girl with some *secured* fortune. That is the only objection to his marrying your daughter, that

I can conceive, upon our side, though it would not weigh with him for a moment. I understand that business-men in America, as a rule, do not make settlements on their daughters when they marry?"

"That is so. But—" Here he paused, then went on. "We need not enter upon that matter. I trust Sir Mordaunt's feelings are not as deeply engaged as you imagine. I trust separation for a year will effectually cure him, and prevent this folly going any further. Clare knows my views on the subject; she has never admitted that she likes your nephew more than as a friend. Now, then, with a little tact, a little firmness, it seems to me the thing may be nipped in the bud."

"I am afraid it is beyond the bud stage. Shall you forbid their corresponding?"

"Forbid? No, indeed, that would be the worst course. I shall tell Sir Mordaunt frankly that I cannot ask him to Pittsburg, and that I do not wish him and Clare to meet for the present. In the summer I shall take the best cottage I can find at Newport, and entertain there, and have a yacht, and let my girl have a good time. It will be strange if some fine young fellow there can't make her forget this fancy —if she really *has* any fancy for your nephew.'

Mrs. Frampton did not think it would be at all strange, but she held her peace. She believed this to be more than "a fancy" on the girl's part. There was, however, the fact, so difficult to explain, that she still refused to bind herself by any pledge. She told Mordaunt she liked him "awfully," but—but—she was not sure of herself; and then "pap-pa" would offer so many objections. In short, as his aunt knew, he had been again refused. Nevertheless, a strong impression remained on Mrs. Frampton's mind, that this was by no means final; and that clever lady had now hoped, but failed, by a *coup de main*, to wrench from Mr. Planter some avowal of what he would do for his daughter if, as Mrs. Frampton put it to Grace, "the worst comes to the worst."

To the young man, the worst—as it seemed to him, at least—had come, when he held Clare's hand for the last time, in the garden, the morning of her departure.

"You will forget all about me, and be snapped up by some New York dude—I know you will," he said. "A whole year without seeing you! It is too awful!"

"You said something about writing to me," she observed, with a smile. "How can I possibly forget you, if I have to answer your letters? Besides, I have your photograph."

"But you wouldn't give me yours."

"Oh! American girls don't give their photographs, unless—their position is different to mine. But I shall have that stalwart form, that magnificent moustache before me, on my writing-table, to refer to, in case my memory becomes hazy. I don't see how I can forget you."

She gave a little laugh, which lacked solidity; he looked hurt.

"If you'd give me some sort of promise, if you'd hold out some sort of hope, that in a year's time—"

"Oh! dear, how tiresome you are!" she cried. "Can't you understand; can't you see that only time and separation can show whether I really and truly care for you? care for you enough to run counter to all pa-pa's wishes; dear, good, old pa-pa, whom I hate to grieve? Nothing would justify my doing this, but caring about a man very, *very* much. I do care for you! There, I have said it. But I don't know how much, till I get away from you. When a man is about you, all the time, it is awfully hard to tell exactly how much you care for him. And if my caring doesn't stand this test, depend on it you will be much better without me."

Here Mr. Planter's voice was heard shouting,—

"Clare! Where are you? We are waiting."

Their hands met, and remained clasped a few seconds. Then they turned quickly towards the hotel, where the omnibus was standing, ready laden.

In New York, a fortnight later, on the eve of embarkation, Grace, who had written to announce her engagement to Mrs. Courtly, received the following letter:—

"*May 1st.*

"My dear Miss Ballinger,—Accept my hearty congratulations and best wishes for your happiness. This good news comes to cheer me to-day, when I feel very sad at heart. It was impossible for me to doubt, even on our short acquaintance, that whoever was fortunate enough to win you, would be no ordinary man. I rejoice to learn that you have found one, to whom you can give, not only your whole heart, but your whole respect and admiration. Poor Quintin Ferrars! It would not have been possible for you to do that, under any circumstances, in his case. He is now free from the terrible mill-stone which hung round his neck more than ten years. But of what avail is his freedom? He will never marry again. He understood, after his last interview with you, how utterly hopeless his suit was, and he sailed last month for Honolulu. You may not be aware that he studied medicine in early life, and the circumstance of being left a moderate fortune, combined with his taste for literature, alone prevented his following it as a profession. He is now resolved to devote himself, for some years to come, to alleviating, as far as he can, the condition of the unhappy lepers in that island. I cannot but feel that the change in my cynical and, as many thought, purely selfish, friend, is due entirely to you. You first made him feel the uselessness of his life. If knowing you has led him to experience the most poignant grief and disappointment he has ever known, it has also led to the ennobling and purifying of his character. Therefore you have nothing to regret. He is one of the men who are born to be unhappy. But there is a higher and a lower condition of unhappiness. You have opened the valve of sympathy with the suffering of others; that is more healthy than inhaling over and over again the vitiated atmosphere of personal misery.

"And now I come to a far sadder episode.

"I had planned a party of literary friends to meet a few days since, and, not having seen Mr. Saul Barham since you were here, I wrote to ask him to Brackley. I did not have an answer for several posts, when a letter came from his mother, whom I did not know, at Fellbridge, saying,—'My son begs me to write to you. He is here with us, very sick, and quite unable to write. He was seized with hemorrhage of the lungs, while passing Sunday with us, a fortnight ago, since when, he has not left his bed. He has had two subsequent attacks, and grows daily weaker. I have lost all hope. Knowing what a kind friend you have been to my dear son, I take the liberty of asking if you would come and see him. I think it would be the greatest consolation to him to see you—to see any friend who would communicate with dear Miss Ballinger—before he is taken. Do you know where she is? He talks of her all the time. Even when he is asleep, I can sometimes catch her name upon his lips. You will forgive me, a stranger, for writing like this to you, dear madam, and if you can come here for an hour, I shall thank you from the bottom of my heart.'

"The simplicity and yet reticence of the heart-stricken mother's letter touched me greatly. You can imagine I did not hesitate an instant, but wired to say I would be at Fellbridge the same afternoon.

"That visit was the saddest hour I ever remember, outside the personal troubles I have had in life. The extreme quietude of everything in that little home, from the sternly-sad, self-contained father downwards, affected me far more than any noisy demonstrations of grief would have done. As to the wan, gentle creature who met me at the door, I could only think of Shakespeare's line, 'Dry sorrow drinks our blood.' Her agony was far too deep for tears. When I was admitted to the poor young man's room, I saw at once that he had not many days to live. But the light flickered up in those wonderful eyes of his, as he held out his hand, and thanked me for coming. His first question was for you. Where were you? Had I heard from you lately? I could tell him nothing, except that I believed you to be still in California. Then he asked me to transmit a message to you, whenever I could do so. 'Tell her,' he said, 'that the happier hours of my life I owe to her. Little mother will not mind my saying that. She knows that the first and only love of my manhood was for that noble Englishwoman. If she had returned my love, I should have struggled—fought for life. Perhaps I should have won. As it is, I am glad to go. If it were not for little mother, I should not have a regret. But her love is so unselfish. She has seen my suffering. She has borne my irritability. She knows I shall be happier at rest.'

"I sat with him for some time, his mother beside me, Mr. Barham standing at the foot of the bed. I thought it must wound him that Saul never once alluded to his father—appeared to think that *he* would never feel his son's death. Was this the result of a principle of lifelong suppression on the minister's part? Could it be that I, the stranger, surmised better the intensity of the elder man's feelings than did his dying boy? I know not; I can only say what struck me.

After a while I saw that he was exhausted.

Talking made him cough; and there was a thin red streak on the handkerchief he held to his mouth. 'Would you object to joining us in prayer by my son's side?' Mr. Barham then said in a perfectly unemotional voice. It was the first time he had broken silence, since entering the room. I instantly knelt down, and, taking Saul's hand in mine, bowed my head, while the minister with great solemnity repeated that fine prayer from 'The Visitation of the Sick,' beginning 'O Father of mercies, and God of all comfort.'

"When he had finished, there was silence for a minute or two. I looked up and saw the poor mother's tearless eyes fixed upon her son's. I stooped, as I rose from my knees, and kissed him on the forehead. 'Good-bye,' I whispered. 'Good-bye, for a little while. I shall bear your love to her, and tell her you are gone to await her coming in that glad place where we all hope to meet.' His beautiful eyes alone answered me; his lips moved, but I could not hear what they murmured. And so, afraid of breaking down, I turned and hurried from the room.

"On receiving your letter, I wrote at once to Mrs. Barham. The answer came in a telegram to-day, which I recognize as the minister's wording :—

"'*Saul departed this life at daybreak.*'

"So the aching heart and troubled spirit are at rest; and until death summons the poor father and mother to rejoin their beloved son, they must wander wearily on, bereft of the pride and joy of their life!

"I will not ask your forgiveness for writing at such length. Though knowing the young man comparatively but little, my heart has been deeply stirred. Yours, with much greater reason, cannot fail to be so.

"I am, dear Miss Ballinger,
"Yours most cordially,
"ANNE COURTLY."

This letter affected Grace Ballinger deeply. It was placed in her hand, with a packet of others, as she stepped on board the *Majestic*, on her homeward passage, and she read it as they steamed down the Hudson. Lawrence found her looking very sorrowful, her eyes fixed on the river banks she remembered watching with Saul, in the fog, as they stood on deck together that January morning, less than five months ago.

"Something has troubled you, dear," he said in a low voice, as he put his hand upon hers. "What is it?"

"It is Life," she answered, presently. "Life, and his brother, Death. Read that." She gave him the letter. "I have told you about him. I have told you about both those men. I knew them both but such a short time; yet each interested me deeply, and over each—I cannot understand how or why—I exercised some strange influence. And now it is all over. The book is closed. Poor Saul Barham, with his brilliant gifts and high aspirations, is dead. Quintin Ferrars I am never likely to see again. Perhaps it is better I should not. But of all the memories of America I bear away with me, the most pathetic is that of the minister's small household in New England, as I knew it, with this only son, their idol, now lying in the dust. Can religion like Mr. Barham's bring consolation? I hope so. But that poor mother! I think I will return to America some day, if it be only to see her!"

Nearly a year has passed since then. Between Clare Planter and her English admirer things remain, to all outward seeming, very much as they were. Newport did not produce the results so confidently looked for by her father, nor has New York done so during the past winter. A constant battledore and shuttlecock of letters, the punctuality of the interchange being only broken once or twice, when Mordaunt Ballinger has forgotten to post his letter in time to catch the American mail, never by the young lady's own negligence, has led Mrs. Ivor Lawrence to assure her aunt that she must make up her mind to the inevitable result of the Planters' approaching arrival in England. She pretends that the American girl's liking for her brother having clearly resisted the effect of separation, and the onslaughts of other admirers, has consolidated into a far stronger affection than existed a year ago. She even declares that she perceives in some of the letters Mordaunt has shown her, a covert dread on Clare's part of his constancy being put to too severe a test. But who can tell? This view of the case may be only that of a devoted sister; and Mordaunt's hopes may be dissipated, on the arrival of the Planters in London, "like the baseless fabric of a vision."

THE END.

www.ingramcontent.com/pod-product-compliance
Lightning Source LLC
Chambersburg PA
CBHW021939240426
43669CB00047B/552